IN THE DRIVER'S SEAT

Cynthia Golomb Dettelbach

IN THE DRIVER'S SEAT
The Automobile in American Literature and Popular Culture

Contributions in American Studies, Number 25

GREENWOOD PRESS
WESTPORT, CONNECTICUT • LONDON, ENGLAND

Library of Congress Cataloging in Publication Data

Dettelbach, Cynthia Golomb.
    In the driver's seat.

    (Contributions in American studies ; no. 25)

    Bibliography: p.
    Includes index.
        1.   American literature—20th century—History
and criticism.   2.   Automobiles in art.   3.   United
States—Popular culture.   I.   Title.
PS228.A95D4   813'.03   75-35342
    ISBN 0-8371-8593-9

Library of Congress Catalog Card Number: 75-35342
ISBN O-8371-8593-9

First published in 1976

Greenwood Press, a division of Williamhouse-Regency Inc.
51 Riverside Avenue, Westport, Connecticut 06880

Printed in the United States of America

Permission has been granted to use excerpts from the following:

"A Day with Bo" copyright © 1969 by Victor Hernandez Cruz. Reprinted from
SNAPS, by Victor Hernandez Cruz, by permission of Random House, Inc.

THE BIG MONEY. THIRD IN THE TRILOGY U.S.A. by John Dos Passos.
Copyright by Elizabeth H. Dos Passos.

THE REIVERS by William Faulkner. Copyright © 1962 by William Faulkner.
Reprinted by permission of Random House, Inc.

116125

FOR JOHN

Contents

Illustrations

Preface

A few years ago I taught a course entitled "The Machine That Got Away." The course attracted a large number of aspiring engineers, and their interest in machines, together with mine in literature, resulted in an exciting dialogue on the impact of technology on modern culture. Out of that teaching experience came the idea for this book.

Since technology per se involved too broad a topic, I decided to concentrate on just one machine. It had to be a machine with which I and most Americans had personal, firsthand experience; it had to affect us in a major way and repeatedly appear, both in a real and symbolic capacity, in American literature and popular culture. Obviously, the machine that best fit all three criteria was the automobile. And from obvious insights, it is hoped, not so obvious books evolve.

What first evolved was a staggering collection of references. They proliferated like the proverbial cars on the highway, and I was constantly having to cut back. Among the important works of literature I was unable to include, for example, were: Booth Tarkington's *The Magnificent Ambersons*; William Faulkner's *Sartoris* and *Sanctuary*; Sinclair Lewis' *Dodsworth* and *Babbit*; Theodore Dreiser's *An American Tragedy*; and Arthur Miller's *The Death of a Salesman*. Others I could only mention in passing.

To return to the book I did write, I am indebted to so many people for their assistance: to Cathi Campbell, who typed the final manuscript; to David Galloway who counseled me from Germany—and all over the world; to Roger Salomon and Park Goist who were there when I needed them; and especially to Fred Smith, who gave of his time, insights, patience, and skills in the difficult tasks of organization and writing.

I am also indebted to many friends who took a special interest in what I was doing and generously shared their own ideas and information with me. Among these I would particularly like to thank Doris Goist, Connie Soltz, and Nancy Lampl. Nancy was my constant sounding board, listening to my problems, reading the manuscript as it evolved, lending her own insights and suggestions, and making the book a better one for her efforts.

I am immensely grateful for winning the Ralph H. Gabriel Prize in American Studies, which made this publication possible, and to Park Goist, who suggested that I submit the manuscript in the first place.

Finally, I would like to thank John Dettelbach, who has, with unfailing support and good humor, lived not only with me but with my ubiquitous yellow pad and typewriter. It is to John that I dedicate this book—a fitting tribute to the man who has its contents seared on his brain from innumerable readings, critiques, and trips to the Xerox machine, and is the only one capable of giving me adequate directions to get somewhere in my *real* car.

C.G.D.

IN THE DRIVER'S SEAT

Introduction: Fumbling for the American Dream

In J. D. Reed's *Expressways,* a book of poems about "the big middle of the country seen through a windshield," the automobile provides the connecting link between the work of art and larger phenomena in American culture.[1] The opening poem, "The Reports Come In," for example, places a hayseed Gulliver against a motorized American landscape:

> A country Gulliver
> staked down on these plains,
>
> rusted Kaisers and hot
> Buicks race out my limbs
> trailing dust like overhead shots
> in comic books.
>
> Inspected by grocers
> and tiny druggists,
> I down twenty hogsheads of syrup,
> wagonloads of meat loaf.
>
> The reports come in:
>   young men with .22's
>   blast roadsigns.

mosquito bumps.

a stuffed trout shudders dust
on the patrons of a roadhouse,

and somewhere in the lamplight
my country lurches from
its cot like a combine lurching
over a field of oats,

and scratching in its underwear,
fumbles for a heritage.

Reed's Gulliver—a neo-Swiftian giant with cars racing out
his limbs, and the car radio serving as his nerve and brain
center—exemplifies the raw material of this book: the car as it is
treated in American art and popular culture. My intent is not
merely to accumulate car metaphors or specific automotive
references; rather, as Reed has done in his poem, I wish to
derive from the created work various insights into the role of
the car in American life and thought.

"America," wrote John Jerome, "is a road epic; we have even
developed a body of road art, *Huck Finn* to *The Grapes of
Wrath* to *Easy Rider*, cutting loose a path to the dream."[2] The
following chapters will illustrate and analyze this automobile-
linked dream—and its attendant nightmare—within the context of our "road art." Because the artist's orientation is
humanistic rather than economic or sociological, his view of the
automobile is richer, more complex, and usually more ominous
than historical data alone might lead us to believe. Long before
our current ecological and energy problems, for example, writers like William Faulkner saw the automobile as a catalyst for
crisis in American life. Therefore, to study the car primarily
from the perspective of literature and related art forms is to
give that study a dimension and drama it would not otherwise
have.

Along the lines suggested by Kenneth Burke, I see the
relationship between literature about the car and the car itself

as one of "dialogic encounter," a process of exchange and interaction. Or, as Burke pointed out, mind (as the seedbed of art) does not mirror environment; it engages it, filtering it through its own uniquely constructed form.[3] *In the Driver's Seat* is concerned with engagement, as Kenneth Burke defined it, in two ways. First, in selected examples like Reed's poem, it suggests the interaction between the car(s) in a particular work of art and cars in a milieu external to that art. Secondly, the book as a whole represents an attempt at engagement between the automobile as artistic device and the automobile as a major phenomenon in American culture. Thus, while I have drawn my own hypotheses about the automobile from a body of primarily literary material, I feel that *In the Driver's Seat* has a relevance beyond literary criticism; it also tries to say something, if only tentatively, about the car's role in the larger dream/nightmare patterns dominating American life and thought.

No doubt there are as many interpretations of the American dream as there are people to ponder the question. Whatever the range or expression of those dreams, however, there are certain basic areas from which all Americans seem to derive both their private and communal fantasies. One has merely to dip into American literature, be a Saturday night movie buff, or be a passive observer of advertisements and popular TV shows to arrive at these dream categories: Youth, Freedom, Success, Possession. But dreams, as we know, are double-edged, comprising the negative extension of fear as well as the positive expression of desire. Where positive dream or fantasy breaks down, the threatening underside of nightmare turns up in its place. Hence youth and its innocence drift into the nightmare of aging and the shocks of unplanned-for experience; the dream of freedom is often thwarted by constraint, success by failure, and possession by man's inability to control his possessions. As the most favored—and problematic—offspring of that particularly American union of space, romance, and technology, the automobile occupies a central place in our fantasies as well as in our daily lives. It is therefore not surprising that in a wide variety of American art forms, the car is the metaphor or microcosm of our ambivalent, dream/nightmare experiences.

America's romantic imagination, which produced native Gullivers in Paul Bunyan and John Henry and is implicit in the creation of Reed's Gulliver, has always drawn heroes larger than life. Behind the wheel of a car, every man is like Gulliver, seemingly stronger, more powerful, and more capable of success than his non-motorized or less mobile brothers. Whereas the unique powers of Lemuel Gulliver sprang whole from the pen of Jonathan Swift, standardized multiples of American Gullivers daily roll off the assembly lines in Detroit or Cleveland and into the garages of their human extensions. Like everything else in America, the notion of mastering space and looming larger than life has been democratized and 'simplified'; all it takes, we are made to believe, is the key to the car.

The ironies of giantism, American-style, are clearly evident in Reed's poem. As the ambivalent quality of "The Reports Come In" suggests, reality is not always commensurate with its idealistic conception. The idea of Gulliver, for example, is synonymous with freedom and vastness of space, yet he himself is described as being "staked down." The young men in the poem indicate that America has its potential heroes, but often as not, they have no heroic acts to perform; their journey perilous consists of blasting roadsigns with .22's from the windows of fast-moving cars. Nor has an older generation of "grocers" and "druggists" found a way out of the dilemma that Gulliver presents. Instead of reveling in their conquest, these tradesmen spend their days in awe of—and servitude to—this giant of immense appetite and needs. Thus technology, monumental though its accomplishments may be, does not always elevate the human condition. Rather, as in Swift's *Gulliver's Travels*, technological expertise often reduces humanity to caricature—to the level of comic books and naive bravado. Despite its positive conception, then, the dream seems destined to turn in upon itself, revealing its darker side.

In America, however, the nightmare of experience never totally eclipses the dreams of an earlier innocence; somehow a remnant remains, even in the face of a negating reality. The reality of Reed's Gulliver, for example, is a sad diminution of his symbolic promise. Still, in the end the giant's dormant power and hope stir as Gulliver, like a latter-day Samson, prepares to confront his heritage. The tenacity and strength of America's car-linked dreams are likewise revealed in the darkest of the nightmare selections to follow. Whether we embrace or painstakingly reject the automobile in our dreams, our nightmares, or our art, we only reaffirm its powerful and immensely attractive hold upon us. And like the good "grocers," "tiny druggists," and romantic dreamers that we are, we still prove ready, whatever the cost, to serve and sing of our motorized Gullivers: to love, hate, and be preoccupied with our cars.

NOTES

1.   Louis Simpson, quoted on the back cover of *Expressways* (New York: Simon & Schuster, 1969).

2.   John Jerome, *The Death of the Automobile: The Fatal Effect of the Golden Era, 1955-1970* (New York: Norton, 1972), p. 103.

3.   For an excellent discussion of Kenneth Burke's philosophy of dialogic encounter, see Gene Wise, *American Historical Explanations: A Strategy for Grounded Inquiry* (Homewood, Illinois: The Dorsey Press, 1973), pp. 113-157.

1 | Youth: Dreams of Innocence, Nightmares of Experience

In describing the first car he ever owned, a '42 Plymouth, Mason Williams says, "I did a lot of firsts in that car, my first feel of big time, real life independence . . . my first sallies into neighboring towns, my first Sally in a back seat, and my first drunk."[1] When Williams, a young musician and author, wrote his "*Auto*biography" (italics mine), the car provided the focus for his "coming of age" in America. Behind the wheel, the young man undergoes the "first existential ordeals, crises, and encounters with experience" that constitute his initiation.[2] Williams adds:

> It was also my first artistic statement. I bought everything I could afford from the Sears' Catalogue Auto Accessories Section and put it on the car. . . . It was a jukebox on wheels.

> I also had my first accident in it. (p. 2)

Despite repeated accidents and mechanical problems with those early cars, Williams glories in the experiences they pro-

8

vide. But rumblings of discontent also surface, and in time his pleasure is eclipsed by a mounting aversion. When he finally can afford "a great way to go" (in a Mercedes or Pierce Arrow), Williams' old dream of going goes awry. With almost paranoiac intensity, he decries the fact that "the whole simple concept of going places in a car has become infected with ulterior psychological labyrinths designed to intimidate and robotize us for purposes of control" (p. 24). As the polysyllabic, unnatural diction suggests, Williams feels bewildered and threatened by the problems of driving. Only one alternative remains: "I'm going to walk where I can," he says, "take the bus, skip it, or ride a bicycle. . . . I've always stayed out of bars to avoid trouble, so I'll just stay out of cars, too" (pp. 25-26).

While "Autobiography" is not a distinguished literary achievement, it does provide an important point of departure for the discussion to follow. First, the fact that a man chooses to sum up his life at the age of thirty or so is indicative of the high premium put on youth in America. Like freedom or success or the possession of material things, youth is an American dream—one that Americans venerate, aspire to, and only loosen their grip on with great reluctance. Secondly, Williams' essay illustrates the importance of the automobile in the life of the young and its crucial role in rites of passage or initiation into manhood. As in any culture, American rites of passage demand a confrontation between the innocent individual and certain time-honored experiences, or, as Williams calls them, "firsts." When, in Ihab Hassan's phrase, there is a great "disparity between the innocence of the hero and the destructive character of his experience," the dreams of youth are shattered.[3] Initiation always signals an end to innocence; initiation into a world of restricted opportunity or, worse yet, pain and violence, makes the loss of that innocence a tragedy. Facing his mini-existential crisis with the car, Williams chooses, both literally and figuratively, to walk out. Others, facing larger crises, cope in different though not unrelated ways. Finally, Williams alludes to the increasingly ambivalent role that the car and a car-dominated culture play in the life of the average American. Conflicting feelings about the car echo that older conflict between the American dream and the American experience. By carrying the burden of promises that often as not remain unfulfilled, the car also reaps the blame for failure.

The automobile's role as both preserver and perverter of American youth has fascinated a broad spectrum of artists and writers. In the title essay of *The Kandy*Kolored Tangerine* Flake Streamline Baby,* New Journalist Tom Wolfe examines the youth-oriented phenomenon of car customizing in California. Unprepared for the frantic, half-mad, baroque netherworld he finds, Wolfe begins simply by recounting his experiences: his first sight of a Teen Fair, a surrealistic carnival with customized cars as its focal point; a tour through the glorified body shops that produce these cars; and interviews with the artists and their young apprentices. What emerges from the reporter's introduction to customizing is a distinct bias in favor of the young. To Wolfe, customizing is a chaotic microcosm of the archetypal American dream. It is a dream of freedom, power, rebellion from authority, creative self-expression, and, equally important, a dream of eternal youth and innocence.

Tracing the origins of the new teenage lifestyle that grew up in California following World War II, Wolfe says, "right at the heart of it, of course, was the automobile."[4] Like the flag and "momism" and apple pie, the car takes on values and connotations far beyond its physical function. In Henry Ford's day, the car was praised as the great equalizer; to the young aficionados of car customizing, the automobile is the great differentiator— between themselves and adults. Adults, or, as Wolfe labels them, the "arteriosclerotic old guys," drive the staid "Mondrian solids" straight off the assembly lines in Detroit or Cleveland. Their offspring, alienated from their parents and their establishment values, drive customized and/or hopped-up cars designed on the freer, Dionysiac principles of "loop-the-loop." To the young, these cars mean "freedom, style, sex, power, motion, color—everything is right there" (p. 64).

Despite the presence of "bouffant nymphets in stretch pants" at the Teen Fairs, Wolfe points out that customizing is an essentially all-male world of almost asexual camaraderie. It is the timeless, adolescent milieu of Tom Sawyer and Huck Finn, only now the raft has four wheels, a handsome chassis, and a high-powered motor. Taking the role of the car in still another direction, Wolfe says, "those objects, those cars . . . have to do with the gods, the spirit, and a lot of mystic stuff in the community" (p. 70). Although, curiously, he doesn't make the analogy himself, Wolfe is pursuing a theme in American culture that began with Henry Adams at the dawn of the twentieth century. In his autobiography, Adams records how, as an old man, he went to the Great Exposition of 1900 and tried to comprehend the technological forces and innovations he saw. Adams was most taken by the dynamo and describes how he "began to feel the forty-foot dynamos as a moral force, much as the early Christians felt the cross . . . . Before the end, one began to pray to it."5

To conjure up California—that vast sun and smog-blinded country swaddled in bands of highways and cloverleafs—is to see why cars are America's newest gods. By their omnipresence and indispensability in daily commerce, cars "possess" most Californians. Because the automobile is a central, even exalted element of their culture, Wolfe points out how California children of artistic bent often gravitated to car customizing. Similarly, all teenagers who devote themselves to cars are, says Wolfe—who sounds here like Adams—"absolutely maniacal" and "practically religious" in their devotions (p. 63).

To illustrate the single-minded dedication of the acolyte to his motorized god, Wolfe tells an amusing anecdote about Ronny Camp, one of the kids who spends all his spare time at George Barris' body shop. Previously, Ronny had a job at a service station. He saved all his money and at Barris' shop customized his own car with a fantastic tangerine-flake Kandy Kolor paint job. Then, Ronny made "a triumphal progress back home to Lafayette, Indiana . . . with his grail" (p. 79). Ronny's Chevrolet is his "grail," and customized cars in California have ties with "gods," "spirit," and "mystic stuff." The art of customizing is "like sculpture in the era of Benvenuto Cellini . . . tied up with religion and architecture" (p. 77). By using these religious images and analogies, Wolfe links car customizing to America's hundred-year-old worship of machines. Like all religions and cults, customizing reflected its adherents' need to create form and meaning where, often, none existed and to live out certain fantasies within a ritualized setting. As Wolfe brilliantly points out, "the car in America is half-fantasy anyway, a kind of baroque extension of the ego" (p. 75). To the young, for whom fantasy often looms larger and more important than life, the car is the perfect receptacle for that self-expression and escape from reality.

Customizers express themselves through the artistic principles of form and color. In matters of form, the young choose streamlining. This principle, which in cars serves no function, but "curves around and swoops and flows just for the thrill of it," is exactly what the young, in a state of flux and experiment themselves, can relate to (p. 70).[6] Customizers also modify color. Barris, for example, is probably as well known for his creation of Kandy Kolors as he is for "chopping and channeling" (i.e., streamlining or altering car shapes). Wolfe points out that according to a study on color and color symbolism, certain color preferences are linked with rebelliousness. Predictably enough, these are the same colors used in customized cars—purple, carnal yellow, and various violets, lavenders, and fuchsias (p. 79).[7]

In still another attempt to set itself apart from traditional society, the teenage netherworld of cars has adopted a vocabulary of its own. Wolfe writes, for example, that the kids will often call a particularly baroque or unusual car a "big bad Merc." "Bad" in this instance is a loaded and ambivalent term. The customized Mercury is "bad" because it is an "assault" on the parents and their lifestyle; as an assault, the car is also "good" because the young take pride not only in their art but in their rebellion. In addition to explaining their lingo, Wolfe often picks up the breathless rhythms and truncated phrases of the young and incorporates them into his own prose.[8] At times, Wolfe's device of walking around in his subjects' sandals becomes irritating, but more often than not, it succeeds in doing what it intends—in animating and, at its best, humanizing the people about whom he writes. To Wolfe, these people have a unique corner on a particularly American phenomenon—the love affair between youth-in-rebellion and the car—which they have elevated into a viable vernacular art form.

One aspect of rebellion that Wolfe mentions briefly in *KKTFSB* and develops at greater length in other essays is speeding.[9] Drag racing and stock car and motorcycle racing fascinate Wolfe for the same reasons they have fascinated other Americans, especially the young. Racing and speeding are forms of escape or liberation; they represent ways of breaking away both figuratively and literally from the slower-paced, less adventuresome world of Establishment adults. All over the U.S., in specifically designated areas or wherever they dare, teenagers race. Those who don't race themselves watch and cheer or, what is more widespread, live the racing experience through other means.

One of the most popular and widely read books among young adolescents during the fifties and sixties, for example, was Henry Gregor Felsen's slick novel, *Hot Rod*. Bud, the hero, is an orphan who finds his surrogate home, family, and analyst in racing his "hop-up." The heavy-handed lyricism of Felsen's prose makes the message perfectly clear:

> When he [Bud] was behind the wheel, in control of his hopped-up motor, he was king of the road. When he was happy, his happiness reached its peak when he could express it in terms of speed and roaring power, the pull of his engine, the whistle of the wind in his ears, the glorious sensation of free flight.
>
> When he was unhappy, discontented, moody, the wheel again offered him his answer. At these times there was solace and forgetfulness behind the wheel. The motor snarled rather than sang, speed became a lance rather than a banner, and revenge against trouble was won through the conquest of other cars that accepted his challenge to race. And when he was alone on the road, his car and its speed seemed to remove him from the troubles that

plagued him while his feet had contact with the earth. Once removed from bodily contact with the ground, once in motion, once in a world of his own making, he escaped his troubles and sorrows in speed.[10]

To be a young king or knight in contemporary America, to lift off from the earth and soar free of trouble, *Hot Rod* suggests you go speeding in your car. Although Bud later gets into trouble for speeding and not conforming to traffic safety rules, the incident is less important, in terms of space and level of interest, than the exhilaration of the race and the chase in fast-moving cars.

Youth's preoccupation with cars is evident not only in the books they choose to read, but in the TV programs and films they watch and in the music they listen to. In the popular rock music of the fifties and early sixties, for example, a large proportion of the lyrics deal with cars—with racing, with speeding, and often, with dying. In an essay in *Hardening Rock*, X. J. Kennedy suggests the relationship between music and the latent stirrings of youthful rebellion during this period. With the flowering of rock and roll, Kennedy says, there was "a stirring of discontent, or at least of passive resistance. Protest of a sort informs those hot-rod and drag race ballads. . . . Evidently one way to get the hell out of adult society is to tromp down hard on the gas. A few heroes tromp so hard they escape permanently." If death by car is the hero's reward in these rock ballads, the ones 'fortunate' enough to survive face more depressing prospects later: " 'Gather ye rosebuds'—whiz around, but face that in the end you'll end up in the great American car lot of old age (if you're not lucky enough to die in a drag race first)."[11]

Like car customizing, racing and the songs that deal with it are characterized by a specialized vocabulary. Because of the high percentage of arcane terminology used, representative songs like "Shutdown," "Drag City," "Little Deuce Coupe," and "Dead Man's Curve" are only for the initiated. Traditional society, which allegedly can't decipher argot like "tak it up," "cool shorts," and "declining numbers," is excluded from even the vicarious experience of the race.[12] The world of cars, as one writer has expressed it, is "a secret garden for the urbanized sons of modern technology."[13] Surely, one effective way to keep the garden secret and free of intruders is to camouflage the path of entry by cultivating a jungle of exotic words through which none but the native can find his way.[14] Interestingly, drag-racing ballads that end in death use much less argot. Violence and death, unlike speeding with a happy ending, break down old barriers. Once the nightmare intrudes upon the dream, the idyllic world of youth is no longer inviolate or private; it becomes instead the painful training ground for coming of age.[15]

The work of art that best captures the special ambience of the music of the fifties is George Lucas' 1973 film, *American Graffiti*. Virtually the entire soundtrack is infused with car sounds and music sounds, cars and rock music being the two things that matter most in the exclusively adolescent world of *Graffiti*. The music comes from car radios; Wolfman, the mysterious disc jockey, talks to people in cars; and, of course, a good deal of the music is about cars. When the music and the cars stop and Wolfman is unmasked for what he is—a kindly but befuddled figure growing old and paunchy—the youthful idyll ends. The most poignant moment of the film reinforces that sense of an ending by transforming Kennedy's "car lot of old age" metaphor into a powerful cinematic image: the scene is a wrecked-car lot in the uncertain light of dawn. Despite his victory in a drag race just hours before, John Milner walks through the lot, strangely depressed. Milner, past his teens already, "knows that his only future is in the car graveyard he haunts. One day his shiny yellow deuce coupe will be junked right on top of the legendary '41 sedan he never had a chance to race."[16]

Whereas car customizing, drag racing, and music provide communal rites of passage for the young, Theodore Weesner's first novel, *The Car Thief*, explores a more individualized initiation into selfhood. Weesner's protagonist, sixteen-year-old Alex Housman, has stolen fourteen cars by the time the book opens. In a flashback we see the first theft, which sets the pattern for those that follow. On that night, Alex goes to his first high school dance, alone. Not knowing how to dance, he stands shyly on the sidelines. He stares as if frozen, not daring to react even to himself and invisible to those around him. Lonely and miserable, Alex decides to leave the dance early. Out in the parking lot he steals his first car, a Chevrolet Bel Air with keys in the ignition. Alex's father is a die setter at the Chevrolet plant and the two of them live on Chevrolet Avenue. The fact that Alex steals a Chevrolet is not mere coincidence; it is Alex's way both of defying his background and ties and, at the same time, of admitting their significance to him. Here, Alex says, is where he belongs, where attention must be paid and his identity asserted.

After an evening and, as we learn later, a lifetime of standing on the sidelines—at school, at home where he can observe but not help his father's drinking problem, and socially—Alex reaches out for a chance to be in control of a situation. Repressed and nonviolent by nature, he can only fantasize about being physically aggressive. But as the "urbanized son of modern technology," he can be defiant and self-assertive by stealing a car. Behind the wheel, Alex, for a brief period, is *somebody*, a person in his own right, the image of his father he remembers most fondly from childhood.[17]

In addition to defining, briefly, Alex's self-image, the car allows Alex to escape from that self. Like the movies he always goes to, the car permits him to change character and setting. Unable to face the daily burden of being a nobody in his own school, for example, Alex often drove to smaller country schools in the area. It pleased him to drive and walk among the "unknown and unknowing" students, a hero with his fancy car. Alex "intentionally parked his Chevrolet Bel Air or his Buick Riviera under their eyes, left the car and re-entered the car under their eyes. He was able to see himself in these moments as he imagined he was seen by them, as a figure from a movie, a stranger, some newcomer come to town, some new cock of the walk with a new car, with a plume of city hair."[18] Riding a "coppertone stallion," the intensely lonely adolescent is transformed in his imagination into the mythical American hero; like the film stars who help shape the myth, Alex is the lone and enviable cowboy riding the range.

Soon, however, the euphoric effect of "standing in someone else's body" (a phrase Alex uses later to describe his real sense of loss and alienation), begins to wear off. This identity crisis is signalled by the frequency with which he stares at his reflection in mirrors or store windows, not so much to judge as to corroborate himself as a person. Alex feels trapped between the ambivalent urge to lose himself and to know himself; he is torn between the compulsion to keep stealing and the need to get caught. As the need to get caught grows stronger, Alex commits a series of intentional errors through which the police track him down and have him placed in a detention home.

Upon leaving the home many weeks later, Alex tries to renew his old ties with his mother (long remarried), his younger brother, his father, and even with stolen cars. When these attempts fail to satisfy him, he decides to enlist in the army. By removing himself from stultifying relationships with his family and other people's cars, he can begin to develop on his own. Although Weesner knows that Alex can come of age only when he is able to face reality without stolen cars or the fantasies he creates in them, the role of the automobile in his painful maturing is not to be minimized. Stealing cars has provided him with a way of working out and then exorcising the various images he has of himself. Only by peeling off these masks one by one can Alex get to know the real self underneath.

From Wolfe to Weesner, the dreams, rebellion, and experiences of youth have been set in a rarefied, almost timeless atmosphere peopled only or primarily by the young. In *The Reivers*, a thinly disguised autobiography about his youth around the turn of the century, William Faulkner explores youthful rites of passage as part of a larger historical and cultural phenomenon. The youthful rebellion is still there and so, too, is the romanticism attached to it; but the process and price of eleven-year-old Lucius Priest's initiation is given a more complex and ambivalent context.

For Faulkner's young hero, initiation is synonymous with breaking the rules defining the idyllic world of his childhood.

In Boon Hogganbeck, the childlike man who works for his
grandfather, Lucius has a more than willing cohort and mentor.
Boon, who has no real ties with family or land, finds in the
automobile "his soul's lily maid, the virgin's love of his rough
and innocent heart."[19] When the Priest family is called out of
town to attend a funeral, Boon tries to "seduce" Lucius into
borrowing his grandfather's car and taking off for Memphis.
But by Lucius' own admission, Boon's "elaborate machina-
tions" to convince him aren't necessary. As the narrator (Lucius
as an old man) recounts it, "I know better now of course and I
even knew better then: that Boon's fall and mine were not only
instantaneous but simultaneous too: back at the identical
instant when mother got the message that Grandfather Lessep
was dead" (p. 50). What follows from this "fall" and consequent
dalliance with "non-virtue" is the tale of the reivers. That tale is
the contriving to get away and then the following of the obsta-
cle-laden course into Memphis; it is spending a night and
having a brawl in Miss Reba's whorehouse. The climax of the
adventure is helping Ned, the stowaway coachman, win a horse
race in order to get back the car he had presumptuously swap-
ped for a horse in the first place.

Lucius' first lesson in the facts of life and non-virtue consists of learning to drive his grandfather's Winton Flyer. The
setting for this event is a far cry from the green and innocent
garden of Lucius' earlier perambulations. More than a half-
century later, the narrator recreates the scene for his own
grandchildren:

> We were in a lane now, going fast between Negro cabins,
> vegetable patches and chicken yards, with chickens and
> mongrel dogs leaping frantically from the dust just in time,
> out of the land and into a vacant field, a waste place marked
> faintly with tire tracks but no hooves; and now I recognized
> it; Mr. Buffaloe's homemade motordrome where Colonel
> Sartoris's law [against driving mechanical vehicles inside
> the corporate limits of Jefferson] had driven him two years
> ago and where he had taught Boon to operate an auto-
> mobile. (p. 50)

In the bleakness of this initiatory arena, Lucius tries to drive:

> So I moved under the wheel, and with Boon beside me,
> over me, across me, one hand on mine to shift the gears,
> one hand on mine to regulate the throttle, we moved back
> and forth across that vacant sun-glared waste, forward a
> while, backward a while, intent, timeless, Boon as much as
> I, immersed, rapt, steadying me (he was playing for such
> stakes you see), out of time, beyond it, invulnerable to
> time until the courthouse clock striking noon a half-mile
> away restored us, hurled us back into the impending hard
> world of finagle and deception. (p. 52)

Boon, working hard and intently, is almost snakelike in his
efforts to guide Lucius. He entwines himself over, across, and
on top of the young boy in a kind of sexual embrace. In this
"sun-glared waste," this inversion of Eden, Lucius is Eve to
Boon's Satan, a willing victim for the high "stakes" with which
Boon has tempted him. Despite the real-life contingencies (the
sun bearing down on the desolate area, Boon's selfish motives,
the "impending hard world" outside), the whole initiation has a
fanciful, romantic element to it. Boon and Lucius go through
their stylized, almost choreographed motions like performers
in a ritual. Even the car functions more as symbol than
machine. It is a prop in the hands of the players and therefore
never in real danger, as in the world outside, of becoming a
force beyond their control. The romantic interlude is short-
lived, however; the courthouse clock, passing judgment on the
hour and the deed, thrusts the renegade pair back into reality.
     As effective as this scene is by itself, we cannot understand
its full impact upon Lucius until a parallel incident occurs later
in the book. At this point, Jefferson (Lucius' home) and Memphis are already behind him. Now, in Parsham, Tennessee,
Lucius still has to prove that he can ride Ned's horse to victory,
the one feat that will recoup both the car and the reivers' honor.
Since Boon and the ladies he is travelling with are locked up in
jail, Lucius asks to spend the night before the race at the home
of Ned's acquaintance, Uncle Parsham.

In his brief relationship with Lucius, the kindly and conservative Parsham represents a powerful counterthrust to the irresponsible Boon. Like many of the old black people whom Faulkner depicts, Parsham is at peace with himself, the land which he has known his whole life, and all creatures who naturally belong there. Boon, on the other hand, first appears on the Jefferson scene "created whole and already ten or eleven years old." Not knowing his own parentage or birthplace, Boon takes on the aspect of an artificially manufactured person; he is "a corporation, a holding company" (p. 19).

While Boon develops an obsession with cars—themselves artificially manufactured products—Parsham, fittingly, drives mules. On the eve of the big horse race, Parsham takes Lucius home from the track in his mule-drawn buggy.[20] Echoing Boon's offer made four days earlier, he volunteers to teach Lucius how to drive the buggy. Parsham's simple directive is to treat a mule with honesty and respect, as one would a human being. "All you need to do," he confides to Lucius, "is to tell him with the lines that you know the way too but he lives here and you're just a boy so you want him to go in front" (p. 246). Lucius can understand this and follows through with ease and success. In retrospect, one realizes that learning to drive the car has no human analogue. Consequently, it requires all of Boon's dexterity moving over, across, and onto Lucius' hands to place them where they ought to be. The lesson in the car takes Boon and Lucius around and around, backwards and forwards in an arid, desolate area.[21] They go nowhere and see nothing, yet for this Lucius pays a stiff price. He barters his innocence, his virtue, and his peace of mind for the uncertain rewards of an early initiation. With Uncle Parsham, on the other hand, Lucius drives the mules to a home, human warmth, supper, and sleep; the end of the journey promises not a loss but a rejuvenation of body and spirit.

In sharp contrast to the world that Lucius and Boon have entered together, the atmosphere associated with the mule is serene and uncomplicated by devious ways and dealings. Parsham has no ulterior motive in helping Lucius, while Lucius, for his part, is no longer the Faustus of the piece but gratefully,

almost innocently, the child again. The ride with Boon in the
motordrome and the buggy ride with Parsham, then, are points
of departure for two different worlds. Because the automobile
experience comes first, however, the old world that Parsham
represents can never be viewed by its young protagonist again
with the same kind of complacency. Its foundations have been
shaken by the intrusion of modernity, symbolized here, as it
often is in Faulkner's works, by the car. The narrator, writing
from the vantage point of fifty-odd years, already knows the
extent of that old world's eclipse. He remembers that in 1905
the wilderness had receded only twenty miles from where it
had been between 1865 and 1870. By 1925, however, they
"could already see the doom. [Men] switched off their automobile engines to the sound of axes and saws where a year ago
there had only been the voices of the running hounds." By
1940, they were forced to load everything into pick-up trucks
and drive two hundred miles over paved highways in order to
find enough wilderness; and by 1980, the narrator predicts,
"the automobile will be as obsolete to reach wilderness with as
the automobile will have made the wilderness it seeks" (pp.
20-21).[22]

With full knowledge of the automobile's coming of age and
its own rites of passage and plunder in American life, Faulkner's narrator can look back at the year 1905 and think of his
boyhood experiences with the car in terms of a comical and
romantic idyll.[23] Yet, like youth itself, the idyll must end. As
leader and patriarch of the Priest family and owner of the
misappropriated Winton Flyer, Lucius' grandfather sits in
judgment of Lucius' escapades. Fittingly, Boss Priest's own life
bears witness to the knowledge Lucius must acquire: that
maturity requires the delicate balancing of two often opposing
intuitions. Owning a car is a good case in point. Although Priest
dislikes the automobile for its disruptive and deleterious effect
on the old way of life he loves, he recognizes its import for the
future. Despite his amusing verbal refusal to acknowledge the
machine age, he harbors a "nightmare vision of our nation's vast
and boundless future in which the basic unit of economy and
prosperity would be a small mass-produced cubicle containing

four wheels and an engine" (p. 28). Instead of confining that vision to bad dreams, Priest exorcises the demon; he goes out and buys such a cubicle for himself.

As for Lucius, the old man declares that he must live with himself and the acts he has committed. He must be an adult and a gentlemen, a person who accepts responsibility for his actions and bears the burden of their consequences, "even when he did not himself instigate them but only acquiesced to them, didn't say No though he knew he should" (p. 302). In reverse order, Lucius learns that maturity and leadership consist not merely in striking out on one's own and for the future, but in valuing the old modes of behavior, too. Lucius Priest is the author's ideal hero because, having grappled with the car and with the conflicting values represented by Uncle Parsham and even his own grandfather, he now stands at that point in time and space where past, present, and future impinge on one another.[24] His initiation consists of arriving at that point and keeping all lines of communication open.

The dreams of youth are dreams of "firsts," of overcoming innocence and knowing and doing that which was once forbidden. In many instances, however, those "firsts" are not really first steps in joining adult society, but attempts, often unconscious, to perpetuate the dream of youth in the face of inevitable change and decay. Hassan writes that Americans, "being supremely conscious of youth, have developed that consciousness . . . into a strict ceremonial of which the mandarins are swaddled infants. Children and youth satisfy at once the demands of our past and the hopes of our future. This is our national neurosis, the form of *our recoil from an actual world* that brings Failure, Age, and Death."[25] The arcane worlds of car customizing, hot rodding, and drag-racing, as well as the individual car thefts of Alex Housman, are forms of recoil not only from establishment values, but from advancing age and disillusionment. For Lucius Priest, whose coming of age occurs much earlier in American time, innocence is a fence that must be cleared if he is to get on to greener pastures in the real world. Yet as Faulkner carefully points out in *The Reivers*, rites of passage require an awareness not only of youthful dreams but of painful adult realities. The dream of youth turns to nightmare—as inevitably it must—when that transcendence so determinedly sought by the young is finally achieved. Then the dreamer himself is no longer young or innocent, and the seemingly infinite range of possibility and fantasy dimishes accordingly. The dream also turns, in Dos Passos' phrase, "belly up," when the actual world that youth discovers brings not only the wished-for experiences, but the unplanned-for burdens of failure, age, and death.

A poignant example of dreamers outliving their dreams, of growing out of youth and innocence and mourning all that that loss entails, may be found in Larry McMurtry's *The Last Picture Show*. Sam the Lion, the owner of the town's only cafe, and Genevieve, the cafe waitress, are no longer young themselves. As a way of holding on to the idea of youth, however, they befriend the novel's two teen-aged protagonists, Sonny and Duane. Because the boys are self-appointed orphans choosing to live apart from their parents, Sam and Genevieve take the role of surrogate parents. At one point, Sonny and Duane decide to escape from an intolerable situation in town by taking off in their pick-up truck for Mexico. On the eve of their departure, both Sam and Genevieve, independently of each other, insist on loaning the boys some money. The gesture bespeaks many things: love and concern for the boys; nostalgia for the romance or youthful folly each of them had indulged in once (e.g., Genevieve had gone to Mexico as a radiant young bride); and an attempt to relive youth vicariously by contributing to Sonny and Duane's experience.

After Sonny and Duane had driven out of sight, "Genevieve went over and kicked lightly at the front tire of her Dodge—to her the tire looked low. The boys had made her remember what it was to be young."[26] In the odd juxtaposition of these two sentences, McMurtry suggests the great difference between the young and the no-longer-young: for the young, the car represents an opportunity to break away and be free; for people of Sam and Genevieve's age, the car stands as a mute reminder of a past that cannot be recaptured and a future that promises little. In the older pair's lives, the car is simply the vehicle that gets them to work and home again. Theirs is the less mobile role—symbolized here by the low tire—of a generation whose opportunities have passed. For Sam and Genevieve, as for the town's only movie theater, time is even running out on "the last picture show."

Whereas the automobile conjures up bittersweet memories and regrets for Sam and Genevieve, it opens the floodgates of terror and tragedy for Skipper, John Hawkes' protagonist in *Second Skin*. From the vast tangle of narrative threads that constitutes the opening of the novel, Skipper begins to sort out and painfully stitch together the "naked history" of his life and the role of the automobile (as well as other vehicles) in its tortured shaping.[27] Skipper's memories and dreams of youth center around his mother, his father, and their most important possession, a car. "The seated woman, the dripping machine, the man working his wrist in idle circles," Skipper writes, "this is the vision lying closest to the peaceful center of my childhood" (p. 6). Yet the center is not destined to hold for there are ominous portents, even from the beginning. The "dripping machine," for example, has always served a dual function. On Sunday afternoons it is the family car, ritually washed and then used for a family outing. During the rest of the week, however, the long black limousine, with its shabby interior of red velvet and the smell of dead flowers, is a hearse for his father, the town mortician. Then one day the undertaker takes his own life, and from that moment the car as hearse becomes emblematic of Skipper's blighted life.

Skipper's mother dies a while after his father, at the home of a relative with whom she has been staying. Skipper has a premonition of that death in the back of the hearse "where I instinctively stretched out to await my final vision of that experience denied me in space but not in time" (p. 7). Spared the real-life details of that scene, Skipper fantasizes the final moment. Again there is a car in the picture, this one a "small open yellow machine with wooden wheels, white solid tires, and brass headlamps" (p. 8). There is a driver, too, dressed in the proper cap, coat, and goggles that the early open automobiles demanded. For the woman removed in time and space when she was alive—"a gifted angel in a dreamer's cemetery"—this is the symbolically appropriate vehicle to carry her to her final resting place.

Years later, when a new person enters Skipper's ill-fated family circle, he, too, has ominous affiliations with the automobile. Fernandez, the "hapless Peruvian orphan" who marries Skipper's daughter Cassandra, undergoes

> a triumphant and rebellious change of character in the wedding car (it was his own though he could not drive it, a sloping green-roofed sedan with cracked glass, musty seats, bare oily floors rent and jagged so that the road was clearly visible, the car Cassandra drove that day only with the greatest effort and determination), this then was Fernandez, who caused me, that day, to smile my most perspiring smile for the loss of my dear blonde-headed Cassandra. (p. 4)

The long, convoluted, densely packed statement (only part of it is quoted here) hints at the disturbing complexity and ambiguity of the bridegroom. Alone, he is a small, almost pathetic creature; with the car, another aspect of his personality emerges. In wartime America, the very fact that he owns a car—and one filled with black-market tires besides—is testimony to Fernandez' potency and influence. Furthermore, when the "hapless Peruvian" is inside the car, he inflicts demands on his new bride and intimidates her father, who even feels compelled to smile at his great loss. Yet lurking beneath Fernandez' newly demonstrated power is a strong suggestion of impotence, symbolized by the groom's inability to drive the car and by the crippled condition of the vehicle itself.[28] While Skipper carefully records these facts, he seems powerless either to register their significance or, as in the moments before his father's suicide, to act.

Further into the narrative, Skipper pieces together other details of that unorthodox wedding trip. When Skipper and Fernandez go to pick up Cassandra, who has been dressing after the wedding at the "U Drive Inn," Skipper notes

how carefully, slowly, Fernandez climbed back into the
old Packard which he himself was unable to drive, and
then took hold of the broken door handle and pulled,
pulled with all his might so that the door slammed shut and
the car shook under the crashing of that loose heavy steel.
Another side of Fernandez? A new mood? I thought so and
suddenly realized that the enormous outdated Packard
with all its terrible capacity for noise and metallic disintegration was somehow a desperate equivalent of my little
old world Catholic son-in-law. (p. 117)

Skipper's flash of insight, that the car is the man, breaks important conceptual ground. Like Hawkes (who has known all
along), Skipper now sees Fernandez' car not merely as a vehicle
of transportation, but as his extension and surrogate. The car is
old or "outdated"; Fernandez is "old world." Each is a disturbing anomaly in the contemporary scene. The Packard has a
terrible capacity for metallic disintegration; Skipper suspects
that Fernandez has an equally terrible capacity for human
disintegration. And in time, Skipper's worst premonitions
come true. Fernandez first makes a mockery of his marriage
and then of his manhood. Thus the "little old world Catholic
son-in-law" ends his brief life as a "fairy spic," mutilated and
beaten to death in a stinking hotel room at the hands of a passing
male lover.

On the bleak Atlantic island where Skipper, Cassandra, and
Cassandra's infant daughter, Pixie, go to live some time later,
the nightmare of malevolent people and malevolent cars goes
with them. The queen/madam of this sterile island is Miranda,
a woman who cuts off life rather than nurtures it. (In a typically
sadistic act, she cuts the nipples off Pixie's baby bottles.) Like
the destructive others who precede her in Skipper's life,
Miranda is immediately identified with a car. It is a racing car
that doesn't run, rusting in a garden that doesn't grow: "and in
the rear the widow's little untended victory garden—a few
dead vines, a few small humps in the frost—and, barely upright
and half-leaning against a weed-grown shed, the long-
abandoned wreck of a hot rod—orange, blue, white, no tires,

no glass in the windows, big number five on the crumpled hood" (p. 52).

Later, Miranda will try to detain and seduce Skipper in her "Cleopatra's car" (Skipper's ironic name for it) while his luckless Cassandra is being sexually used by the island boys in Miranda's house. In images symbolically reminiscent both of the hearse of his childhood and Fernandez' car, Skipper describes the interior of the hot rod as he reluctantly climbs inside: "the broken glass on the floor . . . crackled sharply, the springs were steel traps in the seat, the gearshift lever—little white plastic skull for a knob—rose up like a whip from its socket, the dashboard was a nest of dead wires and smashed or dislocated dials. There was a cold rank acrid odor in that wrecked car as if the cut-down body had been burned out one night with a blowtorch" (p. 94). In a parodic inversion of Cleopatra's legendary barge, Miranda's car is just one more of the infinite variety of death-bearing vehicles inhabiting Skipper's world.

After the car is fixed up and running again, Skipper uses it to chase the hot rod of one of the island boys which he thinks is carrying Cassandra as a passenger. The chase, which almost causes Skipper to drive into the sea, is a decoy, a way of diverting him while Cassandra and her lover, Jomo, go off together to the lighthouse. By the time Skipper realizes he has been tricked and gets to the lighthouse himself, it is too late. Like her grandfather and mother before her, Cassandra takes her own life and, supposedly, that of her unborn foetus. As with Fernandez, Skipper is forewarned of Jomo's character by the car he drives:

> It was a hot rod. Cut down. Black. Thirteen coats of black paint and wax. Thick aluminum tubes coiling out of the engine. And in the front an aerial—perfect even to the whip of steel, I thought—and tied to the tip of the aerial, a little fat fuzzy squirrel tail, little flag freshly killed and plump, soft, twisting and revolving slowly in the snow. (p. 78)

Like some mechanical incarnation of a black cat, this vehicle promises to be bad luck for anyone daring to cross its path. But even more disturbing than its blackness or the ominous overtones of the number thirteen is its overtly phallic appearance, characterized by the thick aluminum tubes and the plump squirrel tail on the aerial. The image of the squirrel tail is not merely sexual but deadly, as if, in Hawkes' view, sex or even love is synonomous with destruction. Skipper's tragic flaw is that he sees all the signs but cannot interpret or act on them. Hence, unopposed by Skipper, Jomo will use Cassandra, as he once used the squirrel, to flaunt his maleness like a trophy, even at the expense of her life.

With the death of Cassandra, all of Skipper's reasons for living seem to run out. At this point he is, like so many of the characters in the earlier novels of Hawkes, the child denied his innocence now grown into a man beset by impotence and destructive machines.[29] However, Skipper, unlike his predecessors, has the ability and imagination to transform one extreme to the other: he can metamorphose nightmare into dream. Hence, at the nadir of his fortunes, Skipper transports himself to a "sun-dipped wandering island in a vast baby blue and coral-colored sea" (p. 48); here he shapes a new life for himself that is at once the antithesis and, through the telling of the tale, the intensification of the old.

Whereas the old existence was marked by sterility and death, the new one is a hosanna to fecundity and life. In the old world, Skipper was a passive victim of destructive men and machines. In the new, he is a catalyst for life that flourishes in the absence of machinery. He is the artificial inseminator of cows on the island and the alleged father of Catalina Kate's child. The one machine that does exist on Skipper's island is a water wheel, effectively paralyzed by the thick, green growth around it. As Tony Tanner points out, through this wheel

we may be reminded of all the steering wheels of the many destructive vehicles Skipper has recalled. One gets the feeling Skipper has, as it were, subsumed all these hostile wheels into this one enigmatic water wheel, but on his island the wheel is 'robbed of its power.' It is another example of a predominantly hostile or dangerous shape being transformed, and losing its power for evil, on the magical blue island. [30]

Skipper's creation of his fictive island is synonomous with the creation of a new dream of youth. In art, as ideally in youth, all of the possibilities and alternatives once closed to him are suddenly reopened. But in reopening possibility, Skipper also reopens memory. Hence, a powerful, almost overwhelming counterthrust to the dream in *Second Skin* is the retelling of the nightmare. It is a nightmare within which all the standard expectations or dreams about the car become sharply inverted. Instead of perpetuating and glorifying his youth, Skipper's childhood car is emblematic of the premature death of his youth and innocence, and prototypical of the terrible cars that follow. Instead of playing a role in the moral and puritanical life Skipper unconsciously longs for as an adult, the car is auxiliary to human depravity and evil. Finally, instead of being sleek, shiny vehicles—proud armor for twentieth-century knights— many of the cars in *Second Skin* are in various states of rust, decrepitude, and paralysis. They are extensions not merely of the people who own them but of Skipper (who r1des in all the cars) and of the whole landscape of deterioration which Hawkes evokes as emblematic of the human condition.

From Wolfe's *KKTFSB* to Hawkes' *Second Skin*, the dream of youth and the consequent nightmare of age have come full circle. While Wolfe, Weesner, and Faulkner stop at the threshold of youth's initiation into experience and selfhood, McMurtry and Hawkes take the reader over the edge to provide a glimpse of the world beyond youth. In Hawkes' world, even the notion of innocence is questionable because the nightmares of failure, unsatisfying experience, and death seem to affect everyone in a mechanized universe regardless of age. The only way Hawkes' characters can escape the nightmare is to die or to create and live life over again on a fictive island of rural simplicity. Skipper survives by opting for the island—and the work of fiction. It is not mere coincidence that Hawkes cites Faulkner as one of the literary figures who influenced him most; in his own work, Faulkner foreshadows the immanence of Hawkes' nightmare landscapes and prepares for its alternatives as well. For both authors, the car is a symbol on the landscape of a modernity that is often achieved at the expense of older and better values. By eliminating machines from his imagined tropical island, Hawkes reduces the threat that technology and the modern world pose. His Catalina Kate is as unlikely to live the nightmare of growing rapacious and calculating in a mechanized universe as is Faulkner's Uncle Parsham. If Hawkes' Skipper has come closer than Lucius to the failure, age, and death which inhabit the mechanized adult world, it is only to retreat all the more quickly to his youth-preserving, machineless island; if he has learned earlier—and more tragically—the destructive potential of sick or evil people with menacing cars, it is only to seal off irrevocably the possibility of cars on his tropical island.

In short, both Faulkner and Hawkes have seen the future and learned that it doesn't work.[31] Therefore they have turned elsewhere in their art. While Faulkner alludes to the desecration of a world grown older and more populous with cars than the one described in *The Reivers*, the main thrust of his work is that of a "reminiscence;" it is a nostalgic picture of a bygone, less technologically complex era and of a boy whose life in the novel never goes beyond the age of eleven. Hawkes dwells longer and more painfully on both the real and symbolic role of cars in destroying youthful dreams only to create another more permanent and car-less youth in his mythical place of no place and "time of no time" (p. 162). And it is here that he chooses to leave Skipper at the book's close. Through their art, Faulkner and Hawkes sustain or refashion the dreams synonymous with youth, thereby keeping the nightmare of growing older—and more mechanized—at bay.

NOTES

1. Mason Williams, "Autobiography," in *Flavors* (New York: Doubleday & Co., Inc., 1964), p. 2.

2. A definition of initiation used by Ihab Hassan in *Radical Innocence: The Contemporary American Novel* (New Jersey: Princeton University Press, 1961; Harper Colophon ed., 1966), p. 41.

3. Hassan, *Radical Innocence*, p. 7.

4. Tom Wolfe, *The Kandy*Kolored Tangerine*Flake Streamline Baby* (New York: Farrar, Straus & Giroux, 1965: Pocket Books ed., 1966), p. 71 (hereafter referred to as *KKTFSB*).

5. Henry Adams, *The Education of Henry Adams* (Boston: Houghton Mifflin Co., 1918; reprint ed., Cambridge: Riverside Press, Sentry Books, 1961), p. 380.

6. Once they were given the choice, adults, too, opted for the freer form of streamlining. Wolfe indicates that many years after Barris and Roth pioneered streamlined designs in cars, Detroit adopted them, much to the delight of a buying public that probably never got over its own dreams of youth, freedom, and rebellion.

7. Car colors also provide important clues to the personality of the driver and the function of the car in Vladimir Nabokov's novel *Lolita* and in Mike Nichols' film *The Graduate*. In the former, Clare Quilty, who is in hot sexual pursuit of the nymphet Lolita, most often drives an "Aztec red convertible." In his 1967 film of Charles Webb's *The Graduate*, Nichols has his rebellious young hero, Benjamin Braddock, drive a flagrantly red Alfa Romeo convertible. Benjamin's red car, like Quilty's, figures importantly in his love life.

8. A typical example reads, "You have the kid from the small town in the Midwest who's like the kid from Keokuk who wants to go to New York and live in the Village and be an artist and the like—he means, you know, things around home are but *hopelessly* totally square" (p. 78).

9. See "The Last American Hero" in *KKTFSB*, pp. 105-144, and "The Mild Ones" in *The Pump House Gang* (New York: Farrar, Straus, & Giroux, 1968), pp. 89-94.

10. Henry Gregor Felsen, *Hot Rod* (New York: E. P. Dutton & Co., Inc., 1950), p. 17. (The 1967 edition I read was in its twentieth printing.)

11. X. J. Kennedy, "An Appreciative Essay," in *Hardening Rock: An Organic Anthology of the Adolescence of Rock and Roll*, ed. Bruce L. Chipman (Boston: Little, Brown & Co., 1972), pp. 5, 4.

12.   X. J. Kennedy, "An Appreciative Essay," pp. 49-55.

13.   S. K. Oberbeck, "Uneasy Rider," in *Newsweek*, August 7, 1972, p. 63.

14.   A specialized argot has also been used in songs about the drug culture. Thus, during the sixties the Beatles wrote lyrics about the exhilarating, mindbending effects of drugs in language that was intelligible only to those capable of deciphering the argot (see, for example, "Lucy In The Sky With Diamonds").

15.   By the seventies, Bob Dylan's rock ballad, "Highway 61 Revisited," casts an even gloomier pall on the phenomenon of the car and the highway down which it travels. Rather than glorying in the highway, Dylan suggests that it is a kind of Dantean pathway through Hell where man goes to kill, pimp, and unload stolen goods.

16.   Stephen Farber, film review: "*Graffiti* Ranks With *Bonnie and Clyde*," *The New York Times*, August 5, 1973.

17.   See also Louis Zukofsky's novella, *Ferdinand* (London: Jonathan Cape, Ltd., 1968), Alan Ginsburg's poem, "Wild Orphan," and Jack Kerouac's *On The Road*. Like Weesner's *The Car Thief*, all of these works deal with the theme of the son in search of the father whom he hopes to find or recreate through the automobile.

18.   Theodore Weesner, *The Car Thief* (New York: Random House, Inc., 1967, 1969, 1971, 1972), p. 10.

19.   William Faulkner, *The Reivers: A Reminiscence* (New York: Random House, 1962: Vintage Books, 1962), p. 28.

20.   Going through Parsham today (the original site is now part of the outskirts of Memphis), one can still see the grand but fading remains of the race-track gates described in *The Reivers*. Ironically, but fittingly, one looks past these gates to see the new use to which the land has been put; it is a dumping ground for old, abandoned, and wrecked cars.

21.   In the film version of this scene, Lucius drives the car in a lush green meadow dotted with trees, wild flowers, and contentedly grazing cattle. Despite his wild turns and maneuvers, Lucius manages not to disturb anything; on the contrary, animal and vegetable life seem to welcome the shiny yellow car (color of the wild flowers) into their midst. Nor does Lucius have any difficulty in driving the car. He takes to the wheel naturally and effortlessly as if cars and machines were second nature to him. Hollywood, itself the offspring of modern technology, seems to be flattering its own image or natural place in the garden, to the detriment of Faulkner's original intention.

22.   The intrusive and destructive effect of the forces of modernity

has been a continuing theme in Faulkner's work. The opening of his short story "Delta Autumn" (1940), for example, deals with this same retreating wilderness and the role of the automobile in accelerating the rape of the virgin land.

23.   For a well-argued analysis of *The Reivers* as a "parody of chivalric romance," see Olga Vickery, *The Novels of William Faulkner: A Critical Interpretation* (Baton Rouge: Louisiana State University Press, 1959; revised ed., 1964).

24.   The "grappling" is literal as well as figurative. At one point, the car gets stuck in the mud, "the expensive useless mechanical toy rated in power and strength by the dozens of horses, yet held helpless and impotent in the almost infantile clutch of a few inches of the temporary confederation of . . . earth and water" (p. 87). The reivers try to get the vehicle unstuck, but only a pair of mules—representative of the old way of life—are capable of doing the job.

25.   Hassan, *Radical Innocence*, pp. 38-39.

26.   Larry McMurtry, *The Last Picutre Show* (New York: Dell Publishing Co., Inc., 1966), p. 132.

27.   John Hawkes, *Second Skin* (New York: New Directions, 1963, 1964, p. 9.

28.   In Faulkner's works, as in Hawkes', a character's inability to drive a car is usually indicative of a more pervasive weakness or impotence: see Horace Benbow in *Sartoris* and *Sanctuary*, and Gavin Stevens (as a young lawyer) in *The Town*.

29.   In Hawkes' *The Beetle Leg*, the lives of all of the characters are dominated and crippled by the flawed mechanical monster that is the dam. When "the great slide" (cave-in) occurs ten years prior to the start of the novel, it takes the life of one man and casts the ominous spectre of death and malevolence over the rest of the community. The alien, destructive potential of machines is also dramatically reflected in the Red Devils, a faceless group of leather-jacketed motorcyclists who roar in and out of the narrative, terrorizing the townfolk. The victimizers in turn become victims as the equally malevolent sheriff and his band of citizens cold-bloodedly gun the Red Devils down.

30.   Tony Tanner, *City of Words: American Fiction 1950-1970* (New York: Harper & Row, 1971), p. 224.

31.   This wording is an inversion of Lincoln Steffens' remark about Communist Russia in 1928, "I have seen the future and it works!"

2

Dreams of Freedom, Nightmares of Constraint

From its literary origins in Melville, Whitman, and Poe, the dream of and quest for freedom in America has been cast in a romantic vein. In the popular mind, the myth of freedom is associated with sturdy pioneers in Conestogas, brave men in whaling boats, and at least one irrepressible young boy on a raft. Paradoxically, however, the prospect of striking out for freedom has also aroused within us fears of danger, alienation, and, as Melville understood, even damnation. In his preliminary remarks about Melville, Charles Olson writes:

> I take SPACE to be the central fact to man born in America, from Folsom Cave to now. I spell it large because it comes large here. Large and without mercy: A hell of wide land from the beginning.[1]

Fittingly, because the fact of space and the dream of freedom it spawns come big, they are also fated to die big. The dangers (real or illusory) lurking within space, disillusionment with diminishing space and the nightmare of enclosure, also come "large and without mercy."

Although the footpath and the dirt road as well as the "end-

34

less" expanses of virgin land have been buried, in most cases, under faceless structures and macadam highways, the old romantic dream of pursuing freedom still persists. One of the most lyrical expressions of that pursuit—this time in the car—can be found in Jack Kerouac's *On the Road.* The book's hero, Dean Moriarity (the real life Neal Cassady), races his wheels where his dreams are, and out of a milieu of alienation and malaise, Kerouac, as Dean's companion and chronicler, spins an exuberant, affirmative book. Bruce Cook, writing of the "Beat Generation" in the fifties, says: "No writer better than Kerouac has ever infused travel—simply getting from one place to another—with such a keen sense of adventure. . . . There must be nearly a hundred quotably eloquent examples of Kerouac on the art of travel, and in all of them, there is such freedom, such an obvious feeling of optimism and joy."[2] To Kerouac's characters, driving a car at high speed on the open road is the essential and quintessential American "trip."

In his ambitious, if often flawed work, Kerouac brings together many established strains in American and European literature. *On the Road* is the boisterous American version of genres like the personal confession, the odyssey, and the picaresque novel. In the confessional tradition of Jean-Jacques Rousseau, Kerouac relates his experiences purely, honestly, and if we are to believe him, "spontaneously," without the more formalized technique of a narrative point of view. Kerouac's accounts of his numerous trips across the country, usually by night and with an intuitively sensed edge of terror and uncertainty to them, echo the manic, nightmare qualities of both Melville and Poe.[3] In his exuberance of language and relish for living, Kerouac embodies the positive qualities of Whitman: *On the Road* is the song of himself (and his friends) improvised to the jazz beat.

For Kerouac, who wrote himself into the novel as Sal Paradise, Dean Moriarity is a trip-tic to "things too fantastic not to tell."[4] He is a "long lost brother" of the soul crying out for liberation—and mesmerizing Sal with his cries. Dean was "born on the road when his parents were passing through Salt Lake City in 1926 in a jalopy" (p. 5), early addicted to stealing cars for the "joy" of it, and happiest when on the move, "the one and noble function of the time" (p. 111).[5]

In the trips Dean and Sal take back and forth across the country, Kerouac often casts Sal as Ishmael to Dean's Ahab. "It was drizzling and mysterious at the beginning of our journey" (p. 110), Sal recalls, in words strongly reminiscent of Ishmael's in *Moby Dick*.[6] In images of the sea, Kerouac tells how Dean and his crew "roll" by Pennsylvania Avenue in their "battered boats" (p. 112) and later "roll" into Mobile "over the long tidal highway" (p. 115). On another trip, when Dean and Sal are driving someone's Cadillac from Denver to Chicago, Sal describes the car as "hold[ing] the road like a boat holds on water" (p. 189). Somewhere in Iowa, with Dean speeding and passing cars, Sal has a nightmare vision of crashing in that "magnificent boat." "As a seaman," he explains, "I used to think of the waves rushing beneath the shell of the ship and the bottomless deeps thereunder—now I could feel the road some twenty inches beneath me, unfurling and flying and hissing at incredible speeds across the groaning continent with that mad Ahab at the wheel" (p. 193).

Whereas the *Pequod* plies its course hunting whales, Kerouac's mad crew uses its "big, scarred, prophetic" Cadillac to pick up girls, find kicks, or simply to GO! For Ahab, the real purpose of the whaling voyage is to pursue the mysterious and all-powerful Moby Dick; for Dean, the quest can end only in the discovery of his father, Dean's real and Sal's spiritual father, the "sad and fabled tinsmith" of their minds (p. 148). To pursue Moby Dick is to court disaster; to pursue the father, eternally lost to his offspring, is to be eternally committed to the road. Thus Kerouac's book must end as it begins, with another long journey through the lonely American night.

Despite the dark terror and uncertainty of the quest, there is still an overriding exaltation in *On the Road.* As Sal explains it, even the sinister underside of Dean's personality—his criminal record and his Ahab-like diabolism behind the wheel—was just a "wild yea-saying overburst of American joy, it was Western, the west wind, an ode from the plains, something new, long prophesied, long a-coming" (p. 11). When Dean is driving a car, nothing comes across more clearly than the joy, exhilaration, and freedom of travel. To be on the road driving at high speed is to "zoom," "roll," "ball the jack," "blow the car," "go flying," and "roar on."[7] The verbs tell the story. For Dean and Sal, racing the car through the American night, "the road must eventually lead to the whole world" (p. 189). "The road is life" at its most exciting pitch (p. 175).

Much has been written by Kerouac and others about the relationship between Kerouac's technique of spontaneous prose and the "urgency and continuous flow of music characteristic of jazz improvisation."[8] Urgency, continuous flow, and improvisation are also characteristic of Dean's handling of the car. He is always "in a sweat" either to get somewhere or to keep moving. As the mood strikes him, he performs daredevil tricks—virtuoso extemporizations on the basic theme of getting from one place to another. As there is an underlying discipline or form in jazz improvisation, so there is a pattern in the travels in *On The Road*. Dean and Sal go from east to west and back again and ultimately head south. The East is the beginning, gray, serious, austere, with the ghosts of its Puritan forbears still lingering in its soil and in people like Sal's aunt. The West is freer and more masculine; it is the last frontier, "the fantastic end of America" (p. 70). Travel back and forth across the country is travel in search of the father, the old broken-down Dean Moriarity of whom we hear so much but never find in *On The Road*. When everything between the East and the West gets too difficult to handle, the road leads to the South, the land of magic, warmth, and mystery. The South is also the womb of the continent where Sal and Dean go to be reborn. And to be reborn, for Kerouac, is to begin on the road in a car once more, "dreaming in the immensity of it" (p. 253).

For Jack Kerouac and his beat friends, driving from one end of the country to another and back again is a never-ending, life-affirming process. *On The Road* affirms life, but that affirmation is written with pain as well as pleasure. The pleasure is in the "kicks"; the pain is in the impermanence of the kicks and in an egocentric pursuit of freedom often achieved at the expense of others. Dean, for example, is so intent on going that when Sal gets sick and can't go any more, Dean abandons him. Pain is also pursuing what can never be found—the generation and world left behind, the old Dean Moriarity lost forever to the renegade sons.

In spite of the pain and the frustration, the quest goes on because, like the improvisations of jazz that the movements and tone of the book suggest, "something would come of it yet. There's always more, a little further—it never ends" (p. 199). The open road doesn't always lead to the parking lot, and even if it does, a parking lot presided over by the manic Dean and described in Kerouac's effusive prose is far from a dead end. It becomes, in fact, a microcosm of Dean's "yea-saying," fast-moving world:

> The most fantastic parking-lot attendant in the world, Dean can back a car forty miles an hour into a tight squeeze and stop at the wall, jump out, race among fenders, leap into another car, circle it fifty miles an hour in a narrow space, back swiftly into a tight spot, *hump*, snap the car with the emergency so that you can see it bounce as he flies out; then clear to the ticket shack, sprinting like a track star, hand a ticket, leap into a newly arrived car before the owner's half out, leap literally under him as he steps out, start the car with the door flapping, and roar off to the next available spot, arc, pop in, brake, out, run. (p. 10)

The whole paragraph is angled, turned, stopped short, and accelerated, as if written with a typewriter bolted onto the shaking frames of the cars that Dean parks. For Kerouac, looking at life through the senses and reflexes of Dean Moriarity, everything is GO! Even "working like a dog" in a parking lot has its rewards; it allows Dean to get his hands on cars and, to borrow Olson's description of Melville, "to ride his own space," even if that space is agonizingly foreshortened.[9]

For Kerouac the writer, the car functions as a catalyst. It is not the automobile per se that appeals to him (John Clellon Holmes, a close friend of his, indicates that Kerouac hated to

drive and, like Sal, was often terrified of being in a speeding
car), but what it stands for and triggers in his literary style.[10] In
the late forties and fifties, the car was the modus operandi for
the young, rootless American off on a trip on his own, high on
life. The trip was what turned Kerouac on and what he wrote
about best. The particular quality of Neal Cassady's driving
seemed to affect an important change in Kerouac's writing; it
was during the period in which he knew and idolized Cassady
that Kerouac first disencumbered himself from "architectures"
and "long, intricate Melvillean sentences . . . that got stalled in
the traffic jam of their own rhetoric." He broke free stylistically
and decided to "write it down as fast as I can exactly like it
happened, all in a rush."[11] The first offspring of this marriage of
style and content was *On The Road* in which, like his hero Dean
Moriarity, Kerouac rides his own space, going fast, wild, and
free.

For the vast horizontal dimension of Kerouac's journey in *On
The Road*, the Puerto Rican poet Victor Hernandez Cruz sub-
stitutes a vertical flight back in time and inward to the self.
Whereas Kerouac's spiritual father is Melville, Cruz draws
upon ancient myth and fairy tale for his version of a modern
quest by automobile:

"A Day With Bo"

hey you know where to eat
what time is it.
the white castle
we with strange people.
hamburgers & cokes. right near the train
you all got a car

we left the apartment. to the cold. a gold falcon.
    we went   up streets &
avenues. snow spotted the tar. the bridges. the tunnels.
where we going.
it's a drive-in. drive up, show your lights & some
    chick will come.

look at those red lights. step on it. O we can fly.
you all want to fly. lights went by.
red   blue   yellow.
like a merry-go-round,   out of manhattan   into the
    bronx.
the white castle, like a drive-in movie.
tight-dressed ladies, young & old.
who's going to order.
what you all want.
four hamburgers apiece—
that's sixteen—& four cokes.
ah
are they good hamburgers
naw; fucking horsemeat. they're eighteen cents apiece.
man that's probably cat hive.
shitty bronx cats slain in the back.

the waiter brings the hamburgers, four on a plate.
they wet, man.
some nasty cats.
damn rubber.
how's the coke.
what you want for eighteen cents, people come here from
    all over the
city cause it's cheap.
look, look at that motherfucker—he got ohio plates.
    people come from anywhere
for this bargain.

the car went back thru the streets.
the bronx left where it has always been.
into manhattan.
bellies full of what we wanted—
burgers & cokes.

& eyes that want to get home & fall asleep. [12]

   The quest motif, as old as the grail legend and as romantic as
Sleeping Beauty, has its ironic and parodic counterpart on the

wintry pavements of present-day New York. Cruz begins his tale with the modern version of "once upon a time" ("what time is it") and then lurches into his narrative. Together with other young wayfarers, Cruz rides a "gold falcon" (a low-priced Ford) to the "white castle" (a chain restaurant serving cheap hamburgers). Because the travelers are probably all dark-skinned, the "white castle" has its particular allure and irony; it's the only white castle that will admit them. When you announce your arrival at the castle ("show your lights"), the poet goes on to tell his friends, the princess within ("some chick") will do your bidding. She will bring you "what you all want"—hamburgers and cokes, "fucking horsemeat" for eighteen cents apiece. The wayfarers arrive at their destination, take sustenance, and then, quest completed, head back to Manhattan. Unlike the mythical city or castle that disappears, as it once appeared, in a mist out of nowhere, the "bronx is left where it has always been," a stolid reminder of the concreteness of place.

Despite the vast diminution from ancient myth to modern reality and from quest to car ride, the reader does not leave "A Day With Bo" disheartened. There is, as in the best of Kerouac's prose, a great energy and vitality in the informal, spontaneous quality of the dialogue and in the rapid stop-and-start movement of the poem. More important, the poet is willing to believe that he really is flying a gold falcon to a magical white castle. In the world of the poem, the wayfarers realize another dream all men have: "O we can fly./ you all want to fly." Their sense of excitement and wonder fairly spills over in the expletive "O." Even the drab, urban winterscape is repainted in bright primary colors, "red blue yellow./ like a merry-go-round," while the white castle is "like a drive-in movie," complete with its cast of "tight-dressed ladies, young & old."

The word "old," emphatically placed at the end of the line, is the first hint of reality rearing its ugly head in fantasyland. In the lines that follow, the prosaic realities get more intrusive: "look, look at that mother-fucker—he got ohio plates. people come from anywhere for this bargain." Yet once he has caught the golden ring on his imagined merry-go-round, the poet is reluctant to give it up; he hangs on a while longer by altering his perspective. Since people are Cruz's point of contact with the real world, the poet weakens that link by disembodying and disconnecting those people from their surroundings. The child-like dream turns surreal. Hence the car goes back through the streets seemingly without a driver, while the travelers them-selves are reduced to "bellies and eyes." Because they have been the undeceived participants in the real experience, bellies and eyes want to get home and fall asleep; in sleep, they too can forget what they have borne witness to and merge with the larger dream sustained by the poet's imagination.

For the travelers in "A Day With Bo," the road lacks Kerouac's physical and temporal expansiveness. In place of the whole continent and seemingly limitless time, there is a small portion of the city and of the day. In place of the apple pie and ice cream which grow bigger and more delicious as Sal heads west, there are the sameness and foulness of the poet's white castle hamburgers. As the physical and temporal possibilities narrow, however, the psychic possibilities expand. From the narrow center of the ghetto experience and the brief trip away to another part of the city, there radiate the larger space and freedom of the poem. The main link between the confining monotony of ghetto life and the flight away from it has been the car. Because the car ("gold falcon") has rich associations with myth, fairy tale, and the ancient Midas legend, Cruz's vehicle for physical escape allows him temporal and psychic escape as well.

From Melville and Whitman, the roads promising freedom have branched out in many directions, and Americans in their automobiles have been quick to follow the proliferating sign-posts. Although a chosen few may have gotten where they wanted to go, most have had to reroute or compromise in some way. Despite the drawbacks of reality, however, the dream of freedom survives, and each artist, in his own way, sings of that survival. The dream music is silenced, however, when man or even his imagination can no longer find some form of freedom. Then the open road seals shut and the nightmare of confinement hangs heavy. According to a growing number of sociologists and social historians, a major factor in destroying personal freedom and the promise of the open road has been, ironically, the widespread success of the automobile. Lewis Mumford says that

> as long as motor cars were few in number, he who had one was king; he could go where he pleased and halt where he pleased. . . . The sense of freedom and power remain a fact today only in low-density areas, in the [rapidly diminishing] open country; the popularity of this method of escape has ruined the promise it once held. . . . In using the car to flee from the metropolis, the motorist finds that he has merely transferred congestion to the highway and thereby doubled it. When he reaches his destination in a distant suburb, he finds that the countryside he sought has disappeared; beyond him, thanks to the motorway, lies only another suburb, just as dull as his own.[13]

In literature, as well as in social commentaries like Mumford's, the dullness and deceptive quality of travel in America has been a target of attack. The car and the superhighway and chain motel it has given rise to are amusingly described and criticized in Vladimir Nabokov's *Lolita*. Nabokov's narrator, Humbert Humbert, sums up the effect of these phenomena on the travelers: "We had been everywhere. We had seen nothing."[14] To John Updike, that perception of sameness and psychic confinement engendered by an automotive culture is emblematic of a more widespread decay of basic American values and dreams. In the closing pages of Updike's *Rabbit Redux*, Rabbit Angstrom is driving around aimlessly with his wife, Janice. Somehow Rabbit finds himself on Summer Street where his former mistress, Ruth, used to live. Because the liason with Ruth had once opened up Rabbit's life and stultifying marriage, he now thinks Ruth's street will open onto "a brook, and then a dirt road and open pastures; but instead the city street broadens into a highway lined with hamburger diners and drive-in sub shops, and a miniature golf course with big plaster dinosaurs, and food stamp stores and motels and gas stations that are changing their names, Humble to Getty, Atlantic to Arco. He has been here before."[15]

Whereas Kerouac's and Cruz's run-on sentences are "active" with verbs and fast-paced dialogue, Updike's run-on sentences take on the static quality associated with a predominance of nouns. The style of *Rabbit Redux* reinforces its content, for as Rabbit drives down Summer Street, he is literally beset by a profusion of inanimate things: diners, stores, gas stations, motels, signs. In place of broad, ever-changing vistas, there are only two-dimensional, changeless facades. The open pastures (real and illusory) have been preempted by big businesses catering to an automotive economy and mentality. Hence, the only animals are plastic replicas of the long-extinct dinosaur, the only thing that flows is gas out of a pump. Even the change of names is testimony to a sad diminution of values and opportunity: Humble (a name which suggests a Christian virtue bespeaking poverty) has been changed to Getty (a name identified with an arrogant, unchristian man); Atlantic (an ocean teeming with life and history) is now Arco (a meaningless word for a business conglomerate). In the same way that signs and dehumanized emporiums for selling objects and services clutter Summer Street, the petty, oppressive details of daily living have obfuscated Rabbit's dream of freedom. Indeed, like an aging Huck Finn, Rabbit "has been here before," in spirit if not in fact, and Updike has painstakingly and painfully recorded it all in *Rabbit Redux* and its predecessor, *Rabbit, Run.*[16]

In *Rabbit, Run*, Harry Angstrom at twenty-six is an ex-high school basketball star now mired in the problems of marriage, parenthood, and a tenuous self-image. The book opens on a typical urban/suburban scene. Boys are playing basketball on a makeshift court when a stranger, Rabbit Angstrom, stops by. "It seems funny to them, an adult walking up the alley at all. Where's his car?"[17] The boys define adults like Rabbit as separate, different from themselves. Boys walk. Adults drive. By confronting the boys on their own ground and insinuating himself into their game and then beating them, Rabbit can only upset the natural order of things. The basketball incident is awkward for everyone, and the boys are relieved when "the old man" leaves.

Rabbit goes home to find his slovenly, pregnant wife, Janice, boozing, and their young son, Nelson, farmed out to Rabbit's parents. After quarreling with Janice, Rabbit goes out, ostensibly to pick up the child, the car (left at her parents' house), and a pack of cigarettes. Instead, he gets into the car alone with the intention of never seeing Brewer, "that flowerpot city," again (p. 24). Rabbit feels pot-bound and trapped in Brewer. The big homes here are "fortresses of cement and brick inset with doorways of stained and beveled glass and windows of potted plants" (p. 10). People and light are only grudgingly allowed in and even plants are forced to grow in small, circumscribed areas. Rabbit thinks back, too, to his own youth, when his parents quarreled and "it was as if a pane of glass were put in front of him, cutting off his air" (p. 21).

Updike's protagonist wants to breathe again, to find open spaces and light. He fantasizes about going "south, down, down the map into orange groves and smoking rivers and barefoot women. It seems simple enough, drive all night through dawn through the morning through the noon park on a beach take off your shoes and fall asleep by the Gulf of Mexico" (p. 25). The nonstop hypnotic rhythms of the sentence recreate the smooth rapid journey of his imagination, the easy, magical descent into a Tahiti-like paradise complete with "smoking rivers and barefoot women." It is typical of Rabbit's myopia that in his longings to be free, he telescopes physical space. For this Gauguin of the fifties, tropical paradise is only a night and day's drive away. Surely, Tahiti begins at the Gulf of Mexico!

Rabbit's "image is of himself going right down the middle, right into the broad soft belly of the land, surprising dawn cotton fields with his northern plates" (p. 30). As it was for Dean and Sal in *On The Road*, the South promises to be warm and comforting, a surrogate mother for the renegade son. But this son (unlike the other two) would insulate himself from the pain of rebirth by flaunting his established identity, "his northern plates." The metallic, alien quality of the license plates is the first of many signs that the trip is doomed. Others follow: Rabbit meets a farmer who distrusts him for not knowing exactly where he is headed, and Rabbit's "good airy feeling inside is spoiled" (p. 28). He wants the trip to be idyllic, a dream voyage, but the car radio crackles with advertisements and news flashes—intrusions of the real world, of mundane things. Even the Dalai Lama, that real figure whose myth is more important than his reality, is reported missing. "Where is the Dalai Lama?" Where have the dream, the myth gone to?

When Rabbit gets to Route 1, which *The Saturday Evening Post* has described as going from Maine to Florida "through the most beautiful scenery in the world" (p. 29), Rabbit sees only hot dog stands and other grotesque outcroppings of modern civilization.[18] He tries desperately to plot out his course, but "false intersections with siren voices" cry out to him: and he teeters on the nightmare edge of being lost—or caught (p. 31). In West Virginia, Rabbit stops for coffee at a roadside cafe, a stranger with his northern plates. Having spoken to no one, Rabbit soon leaves the cafe and climbs into the Ford again, "its stale air his only haven" (p. 32).

Soon, however, Rabbit feels the negative effects of being shut in. The road becomes a "black wall wearilessly rising in front of his headlights." Instead of riding down a broad dream landscape, Rabbit is now on a road that "climbs and narrows" and feeds into gothic visions of shadowy "webs," "spiders," "beasts," and "ghosts." But Rabbit's fears, for the moment, are humorously misplaced. He approaches headlights going in the opposite direction and a few moments later sees a number of parked cars. "So the road of horror is a lovers' lane" (p. 33); less humorously, Rabbit's lovers' lane at home has turned into a road of horror.

Rabbit tries to find his bearings, but his tired eyes have difficulty focusing. The red and blue lines on his map are a "net" within which he is caught. Rabbit lashes out at this imagined net like an animal—or an enraged basketball player— clawing and tearing it to pieces. Immediately, he thinks of the farmer again. Decide where you want to go and then go, the old guy had said. Rabbit's destiny and manhood are tied up with taking the car and driving where he wants to go; he must use the map to find a way out of the maze that is his present life. But Rabbit misinterprets the message and destroys the map, thereby destroying, symbolically, his last chance to escape. Inevitably, the car must head home again. Because it is simpler to acquiesce to his instincts, "the trip home is easier. Though he has no map and hardly any gas, an all-night Mobile gas magically appears . . . and green signs begin to point to the Pennsylvania Turnpike. The music on the radio is soothing now, lyrical and unadvertised, and . . . makes a beam he infallibly flies in on. He has broken through the barrier of fatigue and come into a calm flat world where nothing matters much" (p. 35).

The remainder of the novel is anitclimactic; although Updike continues to write in the present tense, as if life itself were a kind of tenuous limbo, the tension slackens. Rabbit had his one big chance and threw it away. The open road and the freedom beyond were there, but the traveler was detoured by psychic as well as physical roadblocks. Defeated by himself and a landscape which, like the car he drives, encapsulates him in a bell jar of foul air, Rabbit heads back to Brewer, his pursuit of freedom absurdly dissipated. In Brewer, Rabbit parks the car in front of the Sunshine Athletic Association, home of Tothero, his former basketball coach. Lying "secure in his locked window hutch," Rabbit relives behind closed eyes the dream he hasn't been able to pursue in real life. He thinks of "lying down at dawn in sand by the Gulf of Mexico, and it seems in a way that the gritty seat of his car is that sand and the rustling of the waking town the rustling of the sea" (p. 37). The irony of that image—an irony lost on Rabbit himself—is that the original significance of the car has been inverted. Whereas Rabbit once thought of the car both as an instrument of escape and as a way of pursuing his dream, he now sees it as the incarnation of the dream itself. Never having made it to the real Gulf of Mexico, Rabbit comforts himself with the idea that the car is that mythical, unreal gulf of his imagination. The tapering off from geographical place to imagined place in the car is symbolic of the tapering off of all of Rabbit's hopes and aspirations once he returns to Brewer.

Rather than return to Janice, Rabbit decides to move in with Ruth, the girl he meets through Tothero. He leaves Ruth's apartment one day to pick up his clothes at home and finds his car waiting for him in Cherry Street: ". . . it is as if a room of a house he owned had been detached and scuttled by the curb and now that the tide of night was out stood up glistening in the sand, slightly tilting but unharmed, ready to sail at the turn of a key" (p. 82). Unlike the allusions to Melville in *On The Road*, Updike's sea images are bitterly ironic. In a town without water, Rabbit fantasizes that his automobile is his ship. At the turn of a key it will "sail," not onto the high seas of adventure, but back to the cluttered, oppressive apartment he has shared with Janice and Nelson. The car "smells secure: rubber and dust and painted metal hot in the sun. A sheath for the knife of himself" (p. 82). For Rabbit the car now represents protection, a way of cabining himself off from a world that is too much with him.

If the car is not destined to make Rabbit free, neither is it destined to insulate him from pain and injury. Rabbit's Ford had been sold to him at a discount by his father-in-law; to make up the difference, Rabbit owes something of himself to his wife and her family. When the new baby comes, and especially after the baby's tragic death by drowning, Rabbit pays with the little bit of freedom he has left. He goes back to Janice and her father gives him a job selling used cars in one of his lots. Both literally and figuratively, the journey has come to an end. The dream road of promise is now a marketable commodity, and Rabbit's job is to sell it to others in the form of used cars. "The open road," as Louis Simpson once wrote, "goes to the used-car lot;"[19] here, the old clunkers with 80,000 miles on them get their speedometers turned back and, with a phony sales pitch thrown in, are unloaded on unwitting buyers. The clunkers won't get very far, nor, Updike is implying, will the pursuit of freedom. The rusting mechanisms of the cars, like the complex mechanics of living in this world, can only conspire to prevent flight and to rob men of their opportunity to be free.

For Rabbit, as for others, the car has proved traitor to its original promise. Instead of opening up space and offering freedom, his car serves only to close in on him. In his attempt to flee south and back in Brewer, he gets bogged down in signs, objects, and daily routines. But this meticulous accumulation of detail fails to provide any meaningful pattern or gestalt to his existence: Rabbit only feels confined and entombed alive by the unsortable clutter around him. When everything gets to be too much, as periodically it does, Rabbit can cope only by running.[20] On the basketball court, running had once made him free. With the playing surface now changed, however, and the once supple legs clogged with fat and advancing age, the old system doesn't work very well.

In the vastness of America's physical space and metaphysical longings, Rabbit's plight is that he can only run—or stop—within the restrictive bounds of his own small community. The rest of the world and the freedom it promises is still out there somewhere. But for Rabbit, as for Kerouac's and Cruz's characters and countless other Americans, it can only be glimpsed as from an automobile on a back country road at night. It can only be seen through a glass, darkly.

NOTES

1. Charles Olson, *Call Me Ishmael* (San Francisco: City Lights Books, 1947), p. 11.

2. Bruce Cook, *The Beat Generation* (New York: Chas. Scribner's Sons, 1971), p. 39.

3. See Herman Melville, *Moby Dick*, 1851, and Edgar Allan Poe, *The Narrative of A. Gordon Pym* (New York: Harper & Brothers, 1838).

4. Jack Kerouac, *On The Road* (New York: The Viking Press, Inc.; Signet, 1955, 1957), p. 10.

5. In Fletcher Knebel's political novel, *Dark Horse* (New York: Doubleday & Co., Inc., 1972), the eleventh-hour candidate for president of the United States boasts a history remarkably similar to Dean's. Eddie Quinn was born on the road in a Model A, hooked early on cars, and happiest when behind the wheel. The candidate's greatest

asset is that he "understands the American voter in terms of his hidden love—his automobile" (p. 10). A politician's dream turns to loser's nightmare, however, when Eddie causes a terrible automobile accident during the last days of the campaign and publicly admits his guilt (p. 10).

6.   "Whenever it is a damp, drizzly November in my soul . . . " then, I account it high time to get to sea as soon as I can" (Melville, *Moby Dick*, p. 1).

7.   Many of these phrases are also part of the lingo of sex and drugs, two areas in which Dean and his crew also seek their kicks and freedom of expression.

8.   Cook, *The Beat Generation*, p. 221.

9.   Olson, *Call Me Ishmael*, p. 13.

10.   John Clellon Holmes, *Nothing More to Declare* (New York: E. P. Dutton & Co., Inc., 1967), p. 83.

11.   Ibid., p. 78.   Holmes goes on to say that Kerouac wrote *On The Road* in two and a half weeks on a roll of shelf paper fed into his typewriter. The original manuscript was a "scroll three inches thick made of one singlespaced unbroken paragraph 120 feet long, and I knew immediately that it was the best thing he had done" (ibid.).

12.   Victor Hernandez Cruz, *Snaps* (New York: Random House, 1968; Vintage Books, 1969), pp. 91-92.

13.   Lewis Mumford, *The Highway and the City* (New York: Harcourt, Brace, & World, Inc., 1963), pp. 234-235.

14.   Vladimir Nabokov, *Lolita* (Olympia Press, 1955; Berkley Medallion Books, 1966), p. 160.   For further indictments of the insular, homogenized quality of travel in America, see Daniel J. Boorstin, "The Lost Art of Travel," in *The Image: A Guide to Pseudo-Events in America* (New York: Harper & Row, 1961), and George Crowther, *Sanitized For Your Protection* (London: Secher & Warburg, 1966).

15.   John Updike, *Rabbit Redux* (New York: Alfred A. Knopf, Inc., 1971; Fawcett Crest, 1972), p. 345.

16.   The last lines of *Huckleberry Finn* are: "I got to light out for the territory ahead of the rest, because Aunt Sally she's going to adopt me and sivilize me, and I can't stand it. I been there before."

17.   John Updike, *Rabbit, Run* (New York: Alfred A. Knopf, Inc., 1960; Fawcett Crest, 1974), p. 7.

18.   The sad diminution from expectation to reality also occurs, as we have seen, in *Rabbit Redux* when Rabbit drives down Summer Street. Memories of Route 1 lend special poignancy to the line in *Rabbit Redux*, "he has been here before."

19.   See Louis Simpson, "Walt Whitman at Bear Mountain," in *At The End of the Open Road* (Middleton, Conn.: Wesleyan University Press, 1960), pp. 64-65.

20.   Running reenacts the traditional American need to escape from something. From Huck Finn to Augie March to Rabbit Angstrom, American heroes keep running.

3

Dreams of Success, Nightmares of Failure

It is the rare anthology of American poetry that does not include Edwin Arlington Robinson's "Richard Cory." Cory was a "gentlemen,"

> And he was rich—yes, richer than a king—
> And admirably schooled in every grace:
> In fine, we thought that he was everything
> To make us wish that we were in his place.
>
> So on we worked, and waited for the light.
> And went without the meat and cursed the bread;
> And Richard Cory, one calm summer night,
> Went home and put a bullet throught his head.[1]

The particularly American aspect of the poem resides in the ironic nature of its success story. In a country where, as Nathaniel Hawthorne implied, wealth is our only rank, Richard Cory ranks at the top.[2] He is "richer than a king" and therefore, by American standards, more exalted than a king, and his subjects pay him appropriate homage. But the achievement of that successful position, like the measured cadences of the poem itself, masks a more destructive potential beneath. As

Norman Podhoretz says with great understatement, "there are prices to be paid for the rewards of making it in America."[3]

The myth of success—the belief that "life in America was a fluid, wide-open race in which everyone competed on an equal basis—winner take all," was at one time, according to Kenneth S. Lynn, "no more than a mirror held up to nature."[4] Although "nature" changed and grew less benign, as well as less natural, the old success myth still survived. The persistent attempt to adapt the earlier myth to a newer technology, for example, is apparent in the writing of utopian thinkers and authors of children's books around the turn of the century. Their heirs, the creators of advertisements, transformed the old idealism and naiveté into a marketable commodity. They added a liberal dose of sex and offered the now complete success package with every automobile they hoped to sell. Salesmen and idealists aside, however, most Americans acknowledge that success and the car are not necessarily synonymous and that, in any case, the American dream of success has always been qualified. From fine arts to the film to the works of our major writers, the emphasis is on the complexities and often bitter ironies of making it in America. Against the shifting landscapes and machinery of the American experience, the theme of "Richard Cory" plays itself out over and over again.

A decade before the appearance of the automobile, Edward Bellamy linked America's burgeoning technology with the myth of success and the achievement of a great society. The "Great Society" in *Looking Backward*, Bellamy's most important work, is predicated on two simple factors, the morally good man and the technically good machine. Bellamy believes that man is inherently good. Therefore he feels that only "the triumph of common sense" is necessary to organize a system that will satisfy everyone's economic needs.[5] Once man is economically secure, contends the author, he will be free and eager to live in loving community with his neighbor. Together, men will create and flourish in the Great Society. Underlying Bellamy's assumption that economic and even social equality will prevail by the year 2000 is his faith that a highly developed technology will be the substructure of that society. "The perfectability of this new system which Bellamy outlines," says Vernon Louis Parrington, Jr., "is the perfectability of the machine. The machine is pictured as the salvation of man and not the force of destruction which Samuel Butler and Mrs. Dodd picture."[6]

The importance of technology in Bellamy's utopia is best illustrated by its obverse. In the opening pages of the novel, Julian West, Bellamy's narrator, uses a parable to illustrate life as it was in the nineteenth century:

> I cannot do better than to compare society as it then was to a prodigious coach which the masses of humanity were harnessed to and dragged toilsomely along a very hilly and sandy road. The driver was hunger, and permitted no lagging, though the pace was necessarily slow. (p. 27)

For well over two pages, West elaborates on this pretechnological image, equating the privileged rich with those who sat on comfortable seats on top of the coach and "could enjoy the scenery at their leisure, or critically discuss the merits of the straining team." But even these passengers were not without worry. The seats, he says, "were very insecure," and once a man toppled off, he was required to drag the coach with the rest. The "apprehension that this might happen . . . was a constant cloud upon the happiness of those who rode" (p. 27). Bellamy goes on to say that in his time,

> it was firmly and sincerely believed that there was no other way in which Society could get along, except when the many pulled at the rope and the few rode, and not only this, but that no very radical improvement even was possible, either in the harness, the coach, the roadway, or the distribution of toil. It had always been as it was, and it always would be so. (p. 28)

While Bellamy's German predecessor, Karl Marx, concentrated on the plight of the working class and the distribution of toil, Bellamy assumed that all these problems would naturally right themselves once "radical improvement" of the harness, the coach, and the roadway was made. Prophetically, Bellamy anticipated the tremendous strides technology would make and the role it would play both in easing human toil and in improving daily existence.

Just as Bellamy compared nineteenth-century society to a "prodigious coach," it is tempting for us to compare twentieth-century society to a sleek automobile, with revolutionary implications for the improvement of man's lot. With power under the hood, need for the human toil that Bellamy describes is eliminated; the driver is no longer "hunger," but man himself. To extend the analogy even further, the automobile will not only liberate man but, by its very advent, encourage the development of roadways. Hence the "hilly and sandy road" will be transformed into smooth macadam highways which will accelerate the process of beneficial change.

Less than a generation after the publication of *Looking Backward*, Victor Appleton, Jr., began churning out his version of success and the machine in the Tom Swift adventure series.[7] Young Tom is not always the adolescent Buck Rogers creating moon rockets before, in real life, the airplane had gotten off the ground. Often, he is the ideal middle-class youth who invents the kinds of machine that, at the time, were already in the planning or operating stage. Utilizing an unbeatable combination of hard work, enthusiasm, patience, and sheer genius, Tom builds appropriate machines for all occasions. Of course, virtue and accomplishment are their own rewards, but Tom (like the Horatio Alger heroes of the preceding generation) also wins praise and material success.

In 1910, when the car in America was still a relatively new and unusual sight, Appleton published *Tom Swift and His Electric Runabout or The Speediest Car On The Road*. Tom reads about the Touring Club of America contest offering a $3,000 first prize for the inventor of the speediest electric car. Although Tom has no car at this point, he is supremely confident that he can build one and that his car will win. From previous experience, Tom's readers know that their hero's confidence is well-founded. All-American boys with all-American goals were bound to succeed; these truths were self-evident, at least in popular literature.

The machine shop where Tom works is his spiritual home. Typically, it is an all-male domain where females (as well as other undesirable types) are forbidden to enter. Here Tom, the archetypal American tinkerer, can translate dream into reality. Hence, from the secret recesses of his shop there soon emerges the electric runabout. Tom "listens to every sound of the machinery, as a mother listens to the breathing of a child," and is terribly proud of his new creation.[8] Once, Tom is knocked unconscious by a set of crossed wires; when he comes to, the first thing he says is: "My motor might have been ruined if that first charge hadn't gone through my body instead of into the machinery!"[9]

Before the actual contest date, Tom has an opportunity to test his car and demonstrate its social and moral worth. The bank where his father works is in danger of failing for lack of funds. Fortunately for all concerned, Tom, by means of his swift car, saves the day. He procures the necessary money elsewhere and delivers it in time to prevent the bank from closing. Speed conquers all. The book ends a few chapters later with the inevitable: in full view of his adoring sweetheart, Miss Nestor, Tom wins the contest and the prize money. He also succeeds in foiling the bullies who tried to sabotage his invention. Generations of school children growing up on Tom Swiftian heroism could not fail to get the message: the young man who can create or master the machine reaps all of life's rewards and has lots of fun and excitement besides.

Despite the vast differences between them, Bellamy and Appleton share a common optimism about the benefits of technology. They idealized the machine at a time when older methods of achieving success or the good life were being questioned. With the continental frontier gone, the unscrupulous robber barons in disrepute, Horatio Alger dead and his particular brand of *Bound To Rise* heroes relegated to nostalgia, the old ways of bringing home the bacon seemed hopelessly outmoded. New ones had to be found. Certainly, the most logical area in which to look for a replacement was technology, which had been responsible for many of the great changes in the first place.

By the second decade of the twentieth century, technology's baby, the car, had become emblematic of success, American style. With Ford's development of the inexpensive Model T in 1908, the car ceased to be a plaything of the rich and became, instead, the great equalizer. Rural farmer and urban business-man, worker and owner alike, could own a car. With a car, life in America was, as Kenneth Lynn had said of an earlier period, a "fluid, wide-open race" in which everyone could compete, and everyone—with the proper hardware—could take a goodly share of the winnings.

In addition to their immense practical advantages, machines like the car also captured the American imagination. Viewing this phenomenon as an outsider, German author Hermann Broch says that there is an "affectionate attitude toward machines which one almost always finds in boys and in young races—an attitude that glorifies the machine and projects it into the exalted and free plane of their own desires and of mighty and heroic deeds."[10] For a "young race" such as America's, whose classics, Leslie Fiedler once said, were most at home in the children's section of the library, machines were natural subjects for a native literature.[11] In the works of our finest authors and artists, the machine would prove to be a force for evil as well as good, but in the popular literature and culture of the early twentieth century, only the good was triumphant. Unhampered by the realities of failure, frustration, and deeds that often turn out less than heroic, America's fictional heroes could, by means of the automobile, especially, live out their wonderful machine dreams.

Dreams as well as practical needs were also the stuff of which machine sales were made. No one understood this better or capitalized on it more than the manufacturers of automobiles and automotive parts. From the very beginning, the auto-mobile industry relied heavily on advertising to create a dream image of both the car and the car buyer. In the sleek world of the advertisement, the owner of a car, particularly an expensive one, was pictured as a man or woman of enviable importance and accomplishment.

One of the most important discoveries was that "six cylinders had sex appeal."[12] The man or woman behind the wheel had a particular allure that was not lost upon the opposite sex. In advertisements and songs about the automobile, the notion of sex appeal, especially the idea that the boy with the car gets the girl, was parlayed into a strong selling point. The lyrics of the early car song, "Love in an Automobile," spell out the kind of attraction cars had and, naturally, extended to their owners:

> When I first proposed to Daisy on a sunny
> summer's morn,
> She replied, "you must be crazy," and she
> laughed all my love to scorn
> Said I, "Now I've hit on a novel scheme,
> which surely to you may appeal
> Say wouldn't you go for a honeymoon in a
> cozy automobile?"
>
> When she heard my bright suggestion, why, she
> fairly jumped with joy—
> Her reply was just a question, "Oh, say, when do
> we start, dear boy?"
> Said I, "You will take 'bout half an hour to pack
> up your things and grip,
> And then 'round the corner we'll married be, and
> will start away on our trip."[13]

The rejected diffident suitor is, both literally and figuratively, in the driver's seat now. By a kind of sympathetic magic, he takes on the forcefulness and appeal of his machine to emerge the victor in the game of love. He sweeps his coy mistress off her feet and onto the seat of the automobile where, under his aegis, they will travel the road to marital bliss.

Romance in the automobile, with the male in a position of power, has also been emphasized in magazine advertisements. Even if the copy devoted itself to the car's mechanical virtues, the pictures or illustrations hinted strongly of the romantic fringe benefits of owning a car. The women, both in and around the cars, were always beautiful, modishly dressed, and terribly smitten with the dashing man behind the wheel. Except for the Hollywood-style beauty of people and setting, the implications of the ads were not all that misleading. In fact as well as in ad man's fancy, the car did wonders for the American male's sex life. It not only helped him get the girl but provided him with a private place to be with her. Straitlaced Henry Ford not withstanding, the car liberalized and radicalized American courtship by taking it out of the front parlor and onto the highways and back roads of the land.[14]

Cars did more, however, than translate the boys-next-door into roving Don Juans. If ads are any barometer of truth, the internal combustion engine mounted inside a handsome chassis is the key to all mythologies of success. No one portrayed this idea more memorably than Norman Rockwell. His illustration of the Overland Four, a four-door sedan of 1919, graphically attests to the message, "You have arrived!"[15] In the center of the ad, a smartly attired, not quite middle-aged couple is sitting with quiet pride in the front seat of a shiny black Overland sedan. In the right foreground, his back partially to the viewer, stands a boy holding a dog on a leash. Both boy and dog stare wide-eyed at the car from their respectful distance. At the left, a senior citizen (a man blessed with wisdom and long years of experience) looks at the front fender admiringly. Even the proprietor of the market in front of which the car is parked takes time out of his busy day to appraise the gleaming sedan. To all prospective buyers, the point is perfectly clear: to buy an Overland is to show the world—and prove to yourself—that you have achieved the good life.

The automotive industry also realized the tremendous market potential of women. Once the car became clean and easy to operate, even the fair sex could be enticed to buy and drive one. Advertising strategy was simple: promise a woman temporary liberation from the home and opportunity for social enrichment and make her *look* good, and she would come running, checkbook in hand. "What more could she ask than a

YOUR point of view of motoring is determined by the car you own: pleasure and comfort are dependent on its year-in-and-year-out reliability. Riding in an

OLDSMOBILE

the machinery is only apparent as an unobtrusive source of power—boundless, yet delightfully responsive. Inevitably the Oldsmobile owner learns to place absolute confidence in his car . . . . and he experiences the real pleasure of motoring.

Four-cylinder cars $2750.   Closed bodies for each chassis.
Six-cylinder cars $4500.   Details sent on request.

OLDS MOTOR WORKS
Lansing, Mich.
Oldsmobile Co. of Canada, Limited, 80 King St., East Toronto, Ont.

He is in the driver's seat—enjoying the "unobtrusive power" of the car and the company of not one but *two* lovely young women. (Courtesy of the Oldsmobile Division, General Motors Corporation.)

Success is—beautiful people, elegant evenings, the Oldsmobile Six Coupe. (Courtesy of the Oldsmobile Division, General Motors Corporation.)

The car as a surrogate bedroom: the concept updated in George Barris'
Love Machine. (Courtesy of Promotional Displays, Inc.)

The *Love Machine*.
(Courtesy of Promotional
Displays, Inc.)

self-driven carriage that emancipated her from household monotony and suburban provincialism. She was better equipped to enter the social sweepstakes than were Empress Josephine, Queen Victoria, or Madam DuBarry."16 And middle-class Josephine, Victoria, or madam, not yet initiated into the trap of suburban carpools, believed the lie: she bought.

Car styles and engineering have changed with the passing years, but human psychology and most automobile advertisements have not. Analyzing the whole phenomenon of car advertising from the vantage point of the seventies, Kenneth Schneider writes:

> Detroit, in alliance with Madison Avenue, could even help mold life styles through manipulating class ("you have arrived!"), sex (with a shapely female on each fender), or psychic insecurity (compensated for by power, speed, comfort, exhibitionism). The definition advertising gave to man emerged right from the basic elements of the strategy. A new car—being modern, being in style, and having a model marginally distinctive from all others— could make a man new again, strengthen his character, give him the lift of renewed membership in the mobile society.17

The psychology of success records a long and impressive first chapter in American literature, art, and popular culture. Untainted by the counterpsychology of failure, men like Bellamy, Appleton, and their contemporaries and heirs in the advertising world exalted the machine—in particular, the automobile—as the prime symbol and means of achieving success in the twentieth century. Apart from utopian fantasies, children's stories, and ad men's dreams, however, success stories relating to the automobile, like most success stories, were always being qualified. In the arena of sexual success, for example, there is often a victim as well as a victor. Abe, the ghetto Black in Hubert Selby's *Last Exit To Brooklyn*, pays for his glamorous bar pick-ups (and the Cadillac he impresses them with) by reducing his own family to a life of poverty and degradation.

Sedan
$1025

Inevitable Success
because of
Greater Beauty - - -
Finer Performance
Lower Price !
Not one - - But All Three

With one swift sure stride, Oldsmobile attains a position of
commanding importance. Here is greater beauty and finer performance—an impressive achievement that becomes doubly
so with the drastic reduction of Oldsmobile prices! In fair-
ness to yourself, your pocket book and your sense of satis-
faction—arrange now to see and drive this new Oldsmobile.

Touring $875; Coach $950; Sedan $1025. Prices f. o. b. Lansing, plus tax.

OLDS MOTOR WORKS, LANSING, MICHIGAN
OLDS MOTOR WORKS OF CANADA, LIMITED, OSHAWA, ONTARIO

OLDSMOBILE
SIX
Product of GENERAL MOTORS

Promise a woman temporary liberation from the home, opportunity
for social enrichment, and make her *look* good—and she will come
running, checkbook in hand, to buy the 1925 Olds Six Sedan. (Courtesy of the Oldsmobile Division, General Motors Corporation.)

Edward Kienholz' *Back Seat Dodge '38* (tableau), 1964. 1938 Dodge, plaster mannequins, chicken wire, artificial grass, fiberglas, flock, and beer bottles, 5'6'' high x 12' wide x 20' long. (From the collection of Lyn Kienholz; photo by A. J. Petersen, Stedelijk Museum, Amsterdam.)

Bonnie and Clyde's death car—a success in its own right. Peter A. Simon, 22, poses with his new used car: the 1934 Ford in which outlaws Bonnie Parker and Clyde Barrow were ambushed and killed. Simon paid $175,000 at auction to its previous owner, who says the car's 169 bullet holes earned him more than $2 million in exhibition fees over 39 years. (Used with permission of Wide World Photos, Inc.)

More common still, the girl in the back seat is the victim. When the male does the "driving" (car as vehicle, car as penis), the more passive female is usually exploited. Even the nostalgic complacency of the 1970 musical, *Grease*, is disturbed by the audience's awareness that what at least one high-school girl gets out of back seat sex is an unwanted pregnancy.

In Edward Kienholz's life-sized sculpture, *Back Seat Dodge—'38*, the girl-as-victim theme is far more luridly depicted.[18] Kienholz is saying that in the forties, cars like the one he has used didn't produce "love children" but "abortions and tears" instead.[19] The tacky unpleasantness of back seat sex is emphasized by the squat, sinister look of the car. Kienholz has foreshortened the front portion of the vehicle, thereby focusing attention on the awkward, almost painful positions of the "lovers" in back. Only the bottom half of the couple is prominent, an insistence on the mechanical rather than the human aspect of love-making. By fitting out the interior of the Dodge with mirrors, Kienholz prevents the complacent viewer from dismissing the artist's work simply as a period piece. The mirrors throw back the viewer's own image, forcing him to become a participant in the present as well as a spectator of the past.[20]

Success may take its vengeance upon others (as Selby and Kienholz indicate) or upon itself. Those who rise highest may also face the most precipitous fall as often the very instrument of their success becomes an agent for failure. In Arthur Penn's popular film, *Bonnie and Clyde*, for example, the automobile functions in this double-edged capacity. Initially, it is responsible for Bonnie and Clyde's criminal "success." By their skillful handling and swapping of (stolen) cars, the couple is able to make fast getaways and elude pursuing authorities on the road. A kind of poetic justice prevails, however, because the car is also instrumental in their capture. A police ambush is set up, predicated on the simple notion that Bonnie and Clyde will stop to help a stranded motorist. (The 'motorist' is their side-kick's father, who is currently giving them asylum.) When the couple does stop, the police, hiding in nearby bushes, open fire. In a scene as bloody and violent as anything Bonnie and Clyde ever initiated, the ill-fated pair meet their agonizing end against the backdrop of their automobile.

The ambivalent nature and self-generated destruction of success is also apparent in the works of such major literary artists as Faulkner, Steinbeck, Dos Passos, and Fitzgerald. Each in his own way flays the myth of success and scrutinizes its complex realities; each uses the car as a way of illustrating the promise and then the perversion of the original dream. In Faulkner's *The Town*, for example, the automobile functions on multiple, often ambivalent levels. When Manfred De Spain brings "the first real automobile" into the town of Jefferson, Mississippi, in 1904, he sets off a chain of events that has far-reaching implications.[21] Because there is a town ordinance against driving gasoline-propelled vehicles, De Spain is forced to defend his rights as owner/driver. On the basis of this fight to liberalize the old laws, De Spain becomes "the champion of the new age that had entered Jefferson" (p. 12). In the process, De Spain wins a landslide election for mayor and his own career is secured. Inadvertently, the car becomes the agent for its owner's political success. And since, according to the cliché, "nothing succeeds like success," De Spain soon proves triumphant in other areas as well.

When the earthy and sensuously beautiful Eula Varner, already married to a lowly Snopes, moves to town, De Spain and the Harvard-educated idealist lawyer, Gavin Stevens, compete for Eula's attentions. Typical of his indifference to the new world burgeoning within Jefferson, Stevens does not yet have a car. De Spain, on the other hand, has his red E.M.F. roadster, "that vehicle alien and debonair, as invincibly and irrevocably polygamous and bachelor as De Spain himself" (p. 14). And to De Spain and his roadster (again, car as symbolic penis) falls the plum of Eula Varner Snopes.[22]

Publicly, the wronged husband, impotent Flem Snopes, ignores De Spain's affair with his wife. Privately, he exploits that liaison as a springboard for his own advancement. Snopes uses the job De Spain creates for him (as a way of occupying him

nights) to initiate his long, painstaking climb through all levels
of Jefferson society. After eighteen years of hard work, devious
dealings, and blackmail, the last of which culminates in Eula's
suicide, the upstart parvenu from Frenchman's Bend gets
where he wants to be. Snopes sacrifices the wife he never really
had for the position he has always coveted—De Spain's position
as president of the Jefferson Bank.[23]

To commemorate the achievement of his long-awaited success, Snopes buys a car. Ratliffe, the itinerant sewing-machine
salesman who knows and understands the people of *The Town*
better than anyone, describes this momentous event:

> Pretty soon Flem owned a automobile. I mean, presently,
> after the polite amount of time after he turned up presi-
> dent of the bank; not to have Santy Claus come all at once
> you might say. It wasn't a expensive car: jest a good one,
> jest the right unnoticeable size, of a good polite unnotice-
> able black color and he even learned to drive it. (p. 352)

The fact that the parsimonious Snopes buys a car in the first
place, as well as the kind of car he buys, reflects his method of
thinking and operating. Since the automobile, almost two
decades earlier, had given De Spain entree to power and
success, Snopes' purchase symbolizes his inheritance of De
Spain's mantle. Still, there are important differences between
the two, differences that are apparent even in the cars they
choose. Whereas De Spain's first car was a sporty red roadster,
"debonair," "polygamous," and emblematic of a man on the
make, Snopes' car is "a good polite unnoticeable black." It is an
essentially sexless vehicle, appropriate to bankers, undertak-
ers, and underworld characters, and Snopes is, in many ways, a
combination of all three. Like the car he now owns, this Snopes
of black and somber demeanor will quietly and unobtrusively
insinuate himself into positions of even greater power in Jefferson. His mechanical brand of success is achieved at the cost of
his human failure.

In *The Town*, then, there are two important automobiles,
and between them stretches the circuitous avenue of Jeffer-

son's history. Because of the roadster's sheer physical presence, as well as the symbolic value it accrues as a "first" and as a political and sexual weapon, De Spain's car is the key initiator of that history. The departure of De Spain's red roadster and the arrival of Snopes' black sedan signal the end of one era and the beginning of another. Whereas De Spain's car still conjures up the romance and flamboyance of an earlier time, Snopes' vehicle is all business; it represents the powerful, inexorable forces of modernity which the author himself views with increasing ambivalence and distrust.

On the farmlands and prairies of America during this same period, the notion of success, even Snopes-style, was at best an idle dream; straightforward determination to eke out a living was the day-after-day reality. But in the late nineteen-twenties and nineteen-thirties, when a terrible drought, coupled with widespread economic depression, hit the small midwestern farmers, even eking out a living became impossible. Given no alternative but to uproot and to plan and dream of a new life elsewhere, virtually whole states poured out on the roads and headed toward California in cars. As it had been since the nineteenth century, California was the frontier, the new Eden, the last outpost of that old American dream of opportunity and the good life. It was a state whose largely vanished past was perpetuated, especially by enterprising salesmen and landowners, in a golden flow of present tense verbs. And hungrily, if apprehensively, the people listened and got moving.

Woody Guthrie's famous folk song, "Goin' Down the Road," sums up the mood, the hope, and the protest of these troubled times:

Well I'm goin' down this old dusty road, road, road
Yes I'm goin' down this old dusty road
Yes I'm goin' down this old dusty road, road, road
And I ain't gonna be treated this way![24]

The remaining lyrics pose an ambivalent alternation between economic fact and dream. Representing the poor and displaced "dustbowl refugee," Guthrie enumerates the minimal physical necessities he and his family must have in order to survive. His children need three meals a day and he needs ten-dollar shoes to fit his feet. Running apace with his physical requirements are certain psychic needs and dreams. He wants to go to an Edenic paradise where nature is never an alien force ("where them dust storms never blow") and grapes and peaches (not the equivocal apple!) grow in lush profusion.

Each stanza ends with the same powerful and prophetic statement; I dare to demand and I dare to dream, Guthrie insists, " 'cause I ain't gonna be treated this way!" The growing fervor of protest reaches a climax in the final stanza in which Guthrie translates his wishes into an activist platform:

> I'm gonna change this damned old world around,
> round, round
> I'm gonna change this damned old world around,
> Yes I'm gonna change this damned old world around,
> round, round
> 'Cause I ain't gonna be treated this way.

The dream that begins here (as it always does in America) with an escape *from* inequity and poverty ends on a more positive, revolutionary note of working *toward* something better.

Of course, the best-known voice of protest for these dust-bowl refugees is John Steinbeck, who immortalized their plight in *The Grapes of Wrath*, a story of hope, despair, and a new messiah for the masses—the automobile. At first, the automobile represents a threat to these people who have always been insular and fearful of strangers. When the eastern owners of the land or, more distantly still, the owners' spokesmen come to ask the tenant farmers to leave, they come, like the sterile aristocrats in Eliot's *Wasteland*, in "closed cars."[25] Wishing to remain aloof from any real contact with the farmers, "the owner men drove into the dooryards and sat in their cars to talk out the windows" (p. 32). Here the automobile is an alien presence, a machine, a monster, a barrier between men. (The bank's tractors that come later to level the land and raze the tenants'

homes are also described as monsters, "snubnosed monsters
. . . raping methodically, raping without passion" (pp. 36, 37,
38).[26] The unyielding metal of the car separates the "soft fingers" of the smooth-talking owner men and the "hard fingers"
of the laboring tenant men. Across the vast social, economic,
and political abyss, symbolized here by the car, the two worlds
cannot make contact.

If the car is a cold impersonal vehicle come to announce the
end of one kind of world, it is also the symbol or promise of a
new one. The owners tell the tenants to "go . . . west to
California" where "there's work" and "it never gets cold" (p.
35). And the tenants, knowing there is no way to stay and still
maintain their human dignity, make plans to go. They take their
pittance of hard-earned money, together with anything they
can barter, and buy a used car—a "jalopy," "rolling junk."

The fictional Joads, like countless real families, take the old
car they have bought and crudely alter it to hold a load of people
and household goods for which it was never designed.[27] The car
then becomes the living nucleus of their rapidly changing life.
On the eve of their journey to California,

> the family met at the most important place, near the truck.
> The house was dead, and the fields were dead; but this
> truck was the active thing, the living principle. The
> ancient Hudson, with bent and scarred radiator screen,
> with grease in dusty globules at the worn edge of every
> moving part, with hub caps gone and caps of red dust in
> their places—this was the new hearth, the living center of
> the family; half passenger car and half truck, highsided and
> clumsy." (p. 108).

With prophetic irony, Steinbeck designates a machine, an
old and battle-scarred automobile long past its prime, as the
new "living principle." The house, the fields, even the men
themselves are suddenly divested of their traditional power
and vitality. The vehicle has even usurped the name of Hud-
son, a major American explorer, and taken over his pioneering

role. But the car at best is a problematical messiah; it promises hope and a new life at the same time that it signifies a measure of human defeat.

The hybrid, uneasy mix of elements that is the car/truck also reflects the hybrid, unsettled quality of its owners. Like their new homes, these people are without classification or a sense of identity. "How can we live without our lives?" the collective consciousness of the migrants wonders. "How will we know it's us without our past?" (p. 96). The terror of flight, even the flight to apparent opportunity and success, is that it uproots living things and clouds with "dusty globules" the image a man has of his past and, consequently, of himself.

There is no alternative, however, no way to hold on to what must be abandoned. Suddenly a frenzy of movement replaces the long hours and dry seasons of watching and waiting:

> "Suddenly they were nervous. Got to get out quick now. Can't wait. We can't wait. And they piled up the goods in the yards and set fire to them. They stood and watched them burning, and then frantically they loaded up the cars and drove away, drove in the dust. The dust hung in the air for a long time after the loaded cars had passed." (p. 96)

While the dust and the old dreams it must bury settle reluctantly into oblivion, the dreamers of new dreams begin in high gear. The Joads, along with other migrant families, are "in flight" away from the past and toward the future, toward, paradoxically, a 'new' Eden. But "flight" is mostly a state of mind, or at best a euphemism, while the seemingly endless road, the overburdened cars, the heat, and the dust are real. And the real problems must be attended to first. Thus, for two days, "the families were in flight, but on the third the land was too huge for them and they settled into a new technique of living; the highway became their home and movement their medium of expression" (p. 178). Although the language here is strongly reminiscent of Christ's resurrection, the statement itself is a curious inversion of the account in the Gospels. Christ was interred for three days and then rose to new heights of glory; these modern Christians fly on the lofty horizons of their dreams and then settle, on the third day, into a pattern of self-immolation and restraint.

Steinbeck weaves and, as we have seen above, reworks the threads of biblical tales into his own narrative. A little further into the journey, the author describes life on the road in the incantatory cadences of an Old Testament patriarch:

> They were not farm men any more, but migrant men. And the thought, the planning, the long staring silence that had gone out to the fields, went now to the roads, to the distance, to the West. That man whose mind had been bound with acres lived with narrow concrete miles. And his thought and his worry were not any more with rainfall, with wind and dust, with the thrust of the crops. Eyes watched the tires, ears listened to the clattering motors, and minds struggled with oil, with gasoline, with the thinning rubber between air and road. Then a broken gear was tragedy. Then water in the evening was the yearning, and food over the fire. Then health to go on was the need and strength to go on, and spirit to go on. The wills thrust westward ahead of them, and fears that once apprehended drought or flood now lingered with anything that might stop the westward crawling. (pp. 215-216)[28]

Minds that once concerned themselves with the broad spectrum of natural phenomena must now constrict their thoughts to fit the "narrow concrete miles" and the alien mechanical matters of oil, tires, and motors. No longer does man fight against nature: no longer does he strive with gods or the cosmic forces of flood and drought in order to survive. Life on the road is a demeaning contest between man and his fallible machine; it has become a struggle, little better than an animal's, for each day's food and water. In counterpoint with the sad diminishment recorded here, however, is an elevation in Steinbeck's tone and phrasing. As in the sentence, "Then health to go on was the need and strength to go on, and spirit to go on," there is a majesty in the cadences and repetitions bespeaking hope and promise rather than despair. The thrice-repeated phrase, "to go on," posits action rather than stasis, a determination to pursue the dream of success rather than fall back and give in to failure.

The long hours of enforced inactivity in the car allow ample time for planning and dreaming. Rosasharn, pregnant with her first child, envisions a whole new life in California. Her husband will study at home, get to be an expert, and then open his own store; the baby will be born in a hospital and wear "catalogue stuff." They'll live in town and maybe even have a car. Pa, the displaced head of the Joad family, dreams of reestablishing his rightful position. He will earn good wages and then buy "a piece a growin' land with water" (p. 207). Al Joad, the sixteen-year-old driver, hopes to work in a garage and get himself a cut-down Ford to "go a-k-yoodlin' aroun" (p. 337).[29] The younger children dream of picking grapes and peaches to eat whenever they want; then, pragmatists at heart, they dream of a drink of water to get them through the hot, dry hours in the car.

Along with dreaming, the car is a place for living—and dying. Steinbeck distills the vast range of human experience that takes place in the vehicle with a beautiful, low-key description of the Joads the night they cross the desert. The young children sleep, the men talk and reminisce, and Connie and Rosasharn make love under the stars. A couple of feet away from the young couple, grandma lies dying and ma, the source of strength, keeps the vigil alone and in silence through the night. In the morning, the Joads can look over the promised land of California. California is a land of plenty but, as elsewhere, there is plenty only for the companies and banks. "The fields were fruitful, and starving men moved on the roads. . . . On the highways the people moved like ants and searched for work, for food" (p. 313). Eden does indeed exist, but its membership is restricted. As the book ends, the journey still is not over. In more desperate straits than ever, the Joads must now take to the road on foot. The car is mired in a bank of mud and there is no money for gas. But the quest for life, opportunity, and perhaps even success still goes on.

The Grapes of Wrath is a polemic as well as a novel, written with the passionate conviction of a man deploring America's attitude toward its poor and dispossessed and crying out for reform, for a piece of the pie. If the Marxist rhetoric has worn thin with the years, the novel itself has not. It stands as a sensitive portrait of families like the Joads who, despite apprehension and hardship, doggedly travel in their worn-out cars toward the elusive promise of something better. [30]

As one of the novel's central images, the car functions both in a real and symbolic capacity. In the narrative, it is a vehicle of transportation, the Conestoga wagon of the twentieth century; within the thematic structure, it is emblematic of the pursuit of opportunity and the hope for a new life. As a dream image, the car promises social and economic liberation, a way out of Egypt and into the promised land. But as Steinbeck indicates, the spectre of Egypt is always with the oppressed, and no overburdened jalopy can change that.

Moreover, the car itself is a stern taskmaster. At the expense of its human cargo, the car (like its predecessor, the Conestoga wagon) must be fed and tended first. Finally, as the story and history demonstrate, the automobile brings its passengers to a more hostile and merciless land than the one they left. Hence, like its hybrid physical appearance, the car/truck evokes a multiplicity of ambivalent feelings in the author. Although he sees it as the motorized extension of traditional American success-seeking, given the experience of the Joads and others, he sharply and ironically qualifies that "success." For Steinbeck, the car represents the strange admixture of success and failure and resilience that is the American experience.

Like Steinbeck, John Dos Passos also draws upon the contemporary world to fashion his art and his polemics. In *The Big Money*, the third volume of his epic trilogy *U.S.A.*, Dos Passos writes of the twenties and thirties, an era when success in America was never more golden, nor failure blacker. In the lives of at least five of his characters, the real-life Henry Ford and Rudolph Valentino, the fictional Margo Dowling and Charley Anderson, and the composite figure called Vag, the automobile plays a key role.

Dos Passos calls his seven-page biography of Ford "Tin Lizzie."[31] In the author's eyes, the man is the machine and it is the machine that turns out the success story, mechanically and irrespective of the human cost involved. Ford becomes a shrewd, rapacious, single-minded giant, dedicated to enforcing his ideas both on his workers and the world. The author recognizes that Ford has built a colossal automotive empire, but like Ford's much-touted "five-dollar-a-day" plan, there were "strings" to that success story—"always there were strings to it." There was Ford's tyranny over other men's lives and morals: "five dollars a day/paid to good, clean American workmen/who didn't drink or smoke cigarettes or read or think" (p. 73). And there was Ford's mania for increased plant efficiency:

At Ford's production was improving all the time; less waste, more spotters, strawbosses, stool-pigeons (fifteen minutes for lunch, three minutes to go to the toilet, the Taylorized speedup everywhere, reachunder, adjustwasher, screwdown bolt, shove in cotterpin, reachunder, adjustwasher, screwdown bolt, reachunderadjustscrewdownreachunderadjust, until every ounce of life was sucked off into production and at night the workmen went home gray shaking husks.) (p. 75)

Henry Ford, the farm boy, had come to the city to make good. But, Dos Passos implies, he never abandoned his rural psychology. If the land could be made to yield more corn, men could be made to yield more work; what did it matter that, in the end, the remains were "gray shaking husks," human husks instead of vegetable? Ford borrowed his methods from Taylor: reduce everything to a science, to a pattern, to an accelerated blur of "reachunderadjustscrewdownreachunderadjust." This remarkable wordstring captures the dehumanizing, desensitizing process of assembly-line production; in the same way that Dos Passos hurries over and blurs the boundaries of words, Ford hurries over the boundaries of human dignity, thereby blurring the necessary distinction between men and machines. As a result, Americans got cheap cars, workers got good wages, and Henry Ford got rich. But, "always there were strings to it."

Still, Dos Passos can't deny the other side of the story, the mythical dream of success-come-true for the boy who once cleaned kerosene lamps and pitched manure on a farm and in 1922 became "the richest man in the world." Dos Passos concludes the section with Ford as an old man, a "passionate antiquarian" who rebuilds his father's farmhouse and makes it "the way it used to be/in the days of horses and buggies" (p. 77). In the end, he builds a monument to the way of life he had almost singlehandedly destroyed.

When Dos Passos treats Ford with brilliant and devastating irony, his purpose is to castigate society as much as the man. The author sees—and deplores—Americans celebrating success and the man who enjoys it, irrespective of the psychic or human price paid. Ford had given America the automobile, and in the eyes of a machine- and success-worshiping public, all else in the saga was dispensable fine print.

Whereas Ford succeeded by providing cars for the masses, the legendary film star, Rudolph Valentino, used cars as a symbol of his superiority to the masses. In a chapter entitled "Adagio Dancer," Dos Passos writes of the young Italian-born Rudolfo Gughelmi, "who wanted to make good under the bright lights." He got his chance, and under the name of Rudolph Valentino he became "the gigolo of every woman's dreams" (p. 206). To enhance his star image, Valentino, the ex-tango dancer, choreographs his public appearances: "He was always getting into limousines or getting out of limousines, or patting the necks of fine horses. Wherever he went the sirens of the motorcycle cops screeched ahead of him" (p. 207). Expensive cars, sleek horses, and motorcycle cops: these were the minimum Hollywood requirements for creating the image of a virile, sexy, powerful, and successful male star. But the limousines and horses, like Valentino's "admirably-tailored dress suits," turn out to be deceptive facades for the "pink powderpuff" underneath. The star who broadcast his masculinity with the appropriate accoutrements turns out to be the man whose first wife divorced him because they had never slept together. The star whose "elegantly molded body" (the human counterpart of his elegantly molded limousines) threw women into a swoon dies at the age of thirty-one because his insides fill up with ugly, corruptive poisons.

Dos Passos bares further ironies. The public that had demanded limousines and horses and had worshiped the image of a Valentino they had helped create shows only fleeting remorse at his death. In New York, for example, where the funeral was held, people went mad with grief, but then "the funeral train left for Hollywood./In Chicago a few more people were hurt trying to see the coffin, but only made the inside pages./The funeral train arrived in Hollywood on page 23 of *The New York Times"* (p. 209).

The shallowness of people's affections and their need to create heroes replete with ostentatious trappings are echoed in the fictional portions of *The Big Money*. Margo Dowling, an aspiring and conniving young actress, has been living in Los Angeles for three years, waiting (as Valentino once did) for her big break. At a garage, one day, she sees a second-hand Rolls Royce with a coat of arms painted on it. Recognizing the Rolls' potential in aiding her image, Margo arranges to buy it. She then has her husband, masquerading as a chauffeur, drive her to work each day in the car.

In the company of others, Margo refers to the Rolls as "the old family bus" (p. 404). In America, a bus is a poor person's car, shared with other poor persons, other odors, other noises, other destinations. A bus passenger is denied his privacy and is often subject to strangers who may be annoying or offensive to him; Margo, in ironic contrast, has her pristine, luxurious "bus" either all to herself or in the company of people *she* chooses. The vehicle goes only where she wants to go, when she wants to go there. Moreover, the phrase "old family bus" conjures up, for those willing to be impressed, a whole fascinating world elsewhere. It allows Margo to assume an impressive status rooted in aristocracy, family ties, and other cars newer and more valuable than this one. The implication that she has a wealthy, supportive family behind her makes her work seem but a trifling pastime or indulgence, instead of the desperate race for survival that it really is. Predictably, Margo's gambit begins to work. People around the movie lot start to notice her and pay more respectful attention. In the gilt and tinsel world of Hollywood where surface impressions dazzle the beholder, Margo shrewdly assesses that in her underplayed but prestigious vehicle she can more readily travel the road to success.

Charley Anderson, another fictional character in *The Big Money*, drives a car not to impress people but to find release from his sense of inadequacy in other areas. Elevated from airplane mechanic (the job he knows and loves best) to executive, Charley founders in a world of women, politicians, and stock manipulations that he doesn't quite understand. Once, after some bad business reverses, Charley decides to drive to Florida for a vacation. With unpleasant memories left behind and his new girlfriend (Margo Dowling in her pre-Hollywood days) alongside him, "driving down was a circus. . . . The car ran like a dream. Charley kept her at sixty on the concrete roads, driving carefully, enjoying the driving, the good four-wheel brakes, the easy whir of the motor under the hood" (p. 369). Charley is happy knowing that his girl is smart and pretty and "crazy about him," and the sense of mastery he feels in the situation is reflected in his skillful handling of the car.[32]

In Florida, one night, Charley is humiliated in a barroom brawl that he initiates. He gets into his car to escape for awhile and salve his injured ego. Charley is drunk and emotionally shaken; almost as if the car were an internalized mirror or alter ego of its driver, the vehicle refuses to perform. "The gears shrieked because he didn't have the clutch shoved out. The car stalled; he started the motor again and immediately went into high. The motor knocked for a minute, but began to gather speed" (p. 376). Determined to reassert his threatened power and masculinity, especially for a politician's girlfriend whom he has cajoled into going with him, Charley races to a railroad crossing. The car stalls on the track, Charley is hit by an oncoming train, and he dies a few days later. The cause of death is peritonitis. It is the death that Valentino suffered and the symbolic death of an America gone crazy with money, power, and all the other trappings of what would prove to be a very elusive "success."

In a country where automobiles are standard equipment for middle- and even lower-class citizens, and chauffeur-driven limousines are synonymous with the rich and famous, the quintessential have-not is the man without any wheels. Dos Passos ends the panoramic sweep of *The Big Money* with a cameo of such a man. His "Vag" (vagrant/vagabond) stands on the edge of town trying to thumb a ride as the fortunate go "hissing" and "slithering" by in their cars and the more fortunate still are borne aloft in a silver airplane. Vag thinks of the whole vast spread of America while he waits, belly tightened with hunger, for a hitch "a hundred miles down the road" (p. 554). The leitmotif of "a hundred miles down the road" (it is repeated three times in three pages) dramatizes human poverty in spatial terms. In a country where, as Charles Olson remarked, the dream of space "comes large and without mercy," the ultimate deprivation is to telescope one's sights, shrink one's horizons, and then have to depend on someone else's wheels to get there. For Vag, the car he does not own or cannot ride in represents a physical hardship as real to him as his hunger. For Dos Passos, the anonymous man without wheels writes "finish" to the era of big money and even bigger successes, the world of each man for himself and the rest of the world be damned.

Just as Vag is a composite of all the deprived in America, so the five characters taken together represent Dos Passos' multiple perspective on the role of the automobile in American life. As a product of mass-manufacture, the automobile makes money and unmakes people. As a powerful machine, dependent on the uncertain skills and emotions of human drivers, the car is a potential instrument of violence and death, while, as a status symbol, it is often accomplice to human lies and deception. Yet, because the car is, above all, a fact and necessity of American life, Dos Passos recognizes that it deprives those who don't have one of their rights and dreams as Americans.

Rather than "swallowing America whole," as Dos Passos does, F. Scott Fitzgerald chooses to carve out a slice at the top.[33] In *The Great Gatsby*, as in his other novels, Fitzgerald deals primarily with the "beautiful people." These people are born to wealth, pay homage to wealth, or acquire wealth in whatever way they can. Despite the differences among them (and the differences, says the author, are legion), the beautiful people share a common love of the good life and an impressive, successful image. Jay Gatsby is a person who acquires wealth, the archetypal image of the self-made man in America. From humble, obscure, and apparently shady beginnings, Gatsby makes his way to a position of eminence in the only slightly "less fashionable" community of West Egg on Long Island Sound. The spoils and trappings of Gatsby's success are all around him: the Norman mansion (an authentic copy), the marble swimming pool, the carefully cultivated blue gardens, the garage full of cars. Like the money that pays for it, Gatsby's world is a product of technology and human manipulation.

One of the most revealing and condemning aspects of Gatsby's manufactured success is his Rolls Royce. Nick Carroway, the narrator and social outsider of the story, describes the vehicle (familiar to all who knew Gatsby) as being of a "rich cream color, bright with nickel, swollen here and there in its monstrous length with triumphant hat-boxes and supper-boxes and tool-boxes, and terraced with a labyrinth of windshields that mirrored a dozen suns. [It was like] sitting down behind many layers of glass in a sort of green leather conservatory."[34] By his hyperbole, Nick damns the car that he is ostensibly admiring. The pragmatist in him recognizes that a car should function as a means of transportation. Gatsby's, however, is too luxurious and ostentatious for merely practical needs. (Built as a touring car, it actually goes no further than New York City, twenty miles away.) Therefore, Nick sees the Rolls as emblematic of the new, money-made Eden, the status symbol par excellence of the fast-moving, free-wheeling society which Gatsby has unwisely chosen for himself.

Nick also sees Gatsby's car as insulating its owner and filtering his apprehension of reality through deceptive mirrors.

Within this domain—an equivocal one, to be sure—Gatsby is king. In the "monstrous length" of the skin-toned car, "swollen" with mysterious boxes, resides the life and power principle defining Jay Gatsby. Although the car, as machine, represents the positive extension of Gatsby's own "peculiarly American . . . resourcefulness of movement" and grace, the car as status symbol is its owner's negative extension. The origin of Gatsby's status is money, money made in a shady past now suppressed. Money has bought Gatsby the car, as it bought him the house, the servants, the style of life he creates. Because the car is the concrete embodiment of that money and a source of power and mobility as well, it becomes the phallic extension of Gatsby, the man. The cream and green Rolls Royce is Gatsby's connection with England (he tells people he went to Oxford) and with New York City (the present source of his money and influence). It is the vehicle that literally brings society to his parties and his badge of identity anywhere. Finally, the car is, in Gatsby's mind, a repository for his future dreams. Secure inside his mobile, moneyed universe, Gatsby can bask in "a dozen suns." For him these suns are concentrated in an idealized image of Daisy Buchanan, his golden girl, his long-sought love, his dream of ultimate success.

When Daisy no longer reflects his dream back to him, Gatsby's artificially constructed world begins to crumble. The turning point occurs the day he confronts Tom Buchanan with his intentions toward Daisy. As the two men argue bitterly in the stifling heat of a New York hotel room, Daisy weakens in her resolve to leave Tom for Gatsby. The issue settled, Tom insists "with magnanimous scorn" that Daisy drive back from the city with her defeated lover. Tom, together with Nick and Jordan Baker, will follow in another car. A few paragraphs later, the reader learns that

the "death car" as the newspapers called it, didn't stop; it came out of the gathering darkness, wavered tragically for a moment, and then disappeared around the next bend. Michaelis wasn't even sure of its color—he told the first policeman that it was light green. The other car, the one

going toward New York, came to rest a hundred yards
beyond, and its driver hurried back to where Myrtle Wilson, her life violently extinguished, knelt in the road and
mingled her thick dark blood with the dust. (p. 138)

In the dust and blood of that tragic moment, the destructive
potential of the beautiful people and their beautiful cars is
realized. For Gatsby, the incident must have been shocking—
not so for Fitzgerald. From the very beginning, he has been
preparing the reader for the inevitability of the fatal accident by
having Nick describe cars (other than Gatsby's) in terms of
death and decay. At first, the connection between death and
the car is a joke. Teasing Daisy and flattering her that she is
missed by her old friends in Chicago, Nick says: "The whole
town is desolate. All the cars have the left rear wheel painted
black as a mourning wreath" (p. 10). Later, Nick and Gatsby
will pass a hearse on their way to New York. At one point, Nick
gives a surrealistic impression of "gray cars crawl[ing] along an
invisible track and giving out a ghastly creak" (p. 23) on the
wasteland landscape of the valley of ashes. In this nightmare
vision filled with images of entropy and decay, the car is the
only machine mentioned. Finally, throughout the book there
are numerous references to careless or drunken driving (see
pp. 54-56, 58-59), all of which suggest both the potential and
imminence of disaster. By insinuating himself into a world
already marked for doom, Gatsby unwittingly invites the same
fate to befall him. And, in time, it does.

Tragedy does not strike Gatsby all at once, however. Myrtle
Wilson's "death car" has not been positively identified and
Gatsby, like a small boy hiding a broken toy, orders his car kept
in the garage. If it escapes detection, Gatsby thinks he will also.
The car's power has been his power; its immunity will be his,
too. A gentleman to the last, Gatsby conceals the fact that Daisy
was driving at the time of the accident. He also may hope,
faintly, that his chivalry will win her back. But in a world that
cannot be concerned with noble acts, Daisy remains with Tom.
Only George Wilson, by birth and station not acceptable to the
knightly code, performs the one exalted, if misguided, act in

the novel. As the wronged party, he kills Gatsby and then, like Richard Cory, takes his own life.

In the wake of Gatsby's rise to success and his ignominious fall, Nick Carroway pays tribute, at the last, to Gatsby's original dream:

> And as I sat there brooding on the old, unknown world, I thought of Gatsby's wonder when he first picked out that green light at the end of Daisy's dock. He had come a long way to this blue lawn, and his dream must have seemed so close that he could hardly fail to grasp it. He did not know that it was already behind him, somewhere back in that vast obscurity beyond the city, where the dark fields of the republic rolled on under the night. (p. 182)

As myopic as Gatsby is in the pursuit of his dream (the dimmed eyes on the Dr. T. J. Eckleburg sign are a constant reminder of this), the vision itself is far-reaching. Gatsby's dream is not, as he once said of Daisy's feelings for Tom, "just personal." It includes, somehow, all of America, both geographically and historically. To Gatsby, the promise of America, like "the old island here that flowered once for Dutch sailors' eyes," had "pandered in whispers to the last and greatest of all human dreams" (p. 182). Gatsby's dream of success, anchored in idealism, friendship, and love (as well as material well-being), is likewise great and far-reaching. Unlike the others in his society who live carelessly and only for the moment, as their reckless handling of cars indicates, Gatsby has a romantic vision that ₁includes the past and the future. Unknown to him, however, the future "is already behind him," and the dream itself has played Pandar once too often to questionable acts and judgments.

In comparing his neighbor to the people around him, Nick once told Gatsby, "You're worth the whole damn bunch put together" (p. 154). The irony of that remark is that, in the end, Gatsby pays for "the whole damn bunch" of their sins. In both a real and symbolic way, the elegy to Jay Gatsby's success has been ground under the wheels of all the cars careening across the pages of the book. Gatsby's own car is singular for embodying both the dream and the nightmare of his life. The custom Rolls Royce that once brought people flocking to his door remains battered and untended (as Gatsby does) in its last hour; the vehicle that encased Jay Gatsby with power now bears silent witness to his destruction.

Success and failure—both the dream and the "foul dust [that] floated in [its] wake" (p. 2)—find their most eloquent spokesman in F. Scott Fitzgerald. In the world of *The Great Gatsby*, a world of mansions and parties and powerful cars, the very stuff of dreams is woven into the daily fabric of people's lives. But there are rents in the fabric, and Fitzgerald is relentless in exposing them. He lays bare the deception and cruelty in human relationships, the careless regard for truth or possession, the gluttonous consumption of luxury that vomits up a valley of ashes in its wake. Into this world comes Jay Gatsby, a man more vulnerable than the rest because his dreams are greater and his instincts more humane.

In the misguided attempt to turn his dreams into the trappings of success and to crown that success with the unworthy Daisy, Gatsby is doomed to fail. Ironically, the setting for Gatsby's undoing is that which once framed his success; the Rolls Royce becomes the "death car" for Myrtle Wilson, and, symbolically, for Gatsby himself. When Gatsby dies, a beautiful dream dies with him. It is the dream that once made America "the fresh green breast of the new world" and made men like Jay Gatsby the starry-eyed inheritors of all its beauty and bounty. Just as the automobile, "a sort of green leather conservatory," ironically reflects and also diminishes the original vision of "the fresh green breast of the new world," so *The Great Gatsby* reminds us that while the dream is inviolate, the business of grasping it is not. Jay Gatsby learns, as Richard Cory and countless others did before him, that the achievement of success demands its ransom and that, in time, the ransom must be paid.

NOTES

1.   Edwin Arlington Robinson, *Children of the Night* (Boston: R. G. Badger & Co., 1897). In 1972, Paul Simon wrote a song entitled "Richard Cory," using Robinson's theme and many of his lines. Simon's work attests to the relevance and timelessness of the original poem. See (Songs of Paul Simon) (New York: Alfred A. Knopf, 1973).

2.   Hawthorne says that poverty in America is felt "more deeply" than when "an hereditary noble sinks below his order," since, with us, "rank is the grosser substance of wealth" (*The House of Seven Gables* [1851; reprint ed., Boston: Houghton Mifflin Co., Riverside ed., 1964], p. 37).

3.   Norman Podhoretz, *Making It* (New York: Random House, Inc., 1967), p. 2.

4.   Kenneth Lynn, *The Dream of Success: A Study of the Modern American Imagination* (Boston: LIttle, Brown & Co., 1955), p. 3.

5.   Edward Bellamy, *Looking Backward: 2000-1887* (1888; reprint ed., New York: New AmerCcan Library; Signet Classic, 1960), p. xxi.

6.   Vernon Louis Parrington, Jr., *American Dreams: A Study of American Utopias* (New York: Russel & Russel, Inc., 1964), p. 74.

7.   "Victor Appleton, Jr.," is the pseudonym for a stable of approximately thirty writers who turned out the Tom Swift series and, under other pseudonyms, other series.

8.   Victor Appleton, Jr., *Tom Swift and His Electric Runabout or The Speediest Car On The Road* (New York: Grosset & Dunlap, 1910), p. 108.

9.   Ibid., p. 105.

10.   Hermann Broch, *The Sleepwalkers* (New York: The Universal Library, 1964), p. 441.

11.   Leslie Fiedler, *Love and Death in the American Novel* (New York: Criterion Books, 1960; Delta Books, 1966), p. 24.

12.   Rudolph E. Anderson, *The Story of the American Automobile: Highlights and Sidelights* (Washington, D.C.: Public Affairs Press, 1950), p. 191.

13.   Alfred R. Dixon, "Love in an Automobile," publ. by Witmark, 1899; quoted in Anderson, *The Story of the American Automobile*, pp. 215-216.

14.   Given the importance of sexual activity in the car, it is no accident that automobile interiors, especially in customized cars, are designed like boudoirs. One of the outstanding entries in Cleveland's

1973 Rod and Custom Show, for example, was a purple car with a sensuously padded interior of white and purple-veined leather. Reminiscent of a decorator-designed den of iniquity, the entry was waggishly entitled, "Statutory Grape." The subject of "Love and the Automobile" has also been dealt with in the February 1973 issue of *Motor Trend Magazine* and in a photo spread in the April 1973 issue of *Playboy Magazine.*

15.   *Literary Digest,* No. 22, 1919; rpt. in Thomas S. Beuchner, ed., *Norman Rockwell: Artist and Illustrator* (New York: H. N. Abram, 1970).

16.   Anderson, *The Story of the American Automobile,* p. 191.

17.   Kenneth R. Schneider, *Autokind Vs. Mankind* (New York: W. W. Norton & Co., Inc., 1971), pp. 179-180.

18.   *Back Seat Dodge—'38* (Tableau), 1964: 1938 Dodge, plaster mannequins, chicken wire, artificial grass, fiberglas, flock, and beer bottles, 5'6" high x 12' wide x 20' long. It is in the collection of Lyn Kienholz.

19.   K. G. Pontus Hulten, *The Machine: as seen at the end of the mechanical age* (New York: The Museum of Modern Art, 1968), p. 183.

20.   Kienholz's theme of copulation in the back seat of an automobile brought bitter complaints from some outraged museum officials. To 'improve' the situation, these officials closed the doors of the car, making provision for them to be opened only at specified times. Kienholz no doubt chuckled, as did others, at what this remedial measure accomplished. It capitalized on the American delectation in voyeurism and programmed pornography so that at the appointed hours, upwards of 70,000 people filed past the tableau to see the sex show inside. It is also interesting to note that in some exhibits of the Kienholz tableau, there were no mirrors. The removal of the mirrors probably represented still another attempt to eliminate spectator discomfort.

21.   William Faulkner, *The Town* (New York: Curtis Publishing Co., 1957; Vintage Books, 1961), p. 14.

22.   Years later, Gavin Stevens will pursue Eula's daughter, Linda, only to lose out again, this time to Matt Levitt, a mechanic in the Ford Agency garage who sports a yellow cut-down racer. Gavin's brother-in-law good-naturedly accuses Gavin of "losing ground" in the battle for the fair sex: "Last time, you at least picked out a Spanish-American war hero with an E.M.F. Roadster. Now the best you can do is a Golden Gloves Amateur with a homemade racer. Watch yourself, bud, or next

time you'll have a boy scout defying you to mortal combat with a bicycle" (p. 187).

23.   When his scandalous affair of eighteen years is finally brought into the open, De Spain is forced to leave Jefferson, thereby breaking down the last barrier to Snopes' rise to the top.

24.   See Appendix for the complete text.

25.   John Steinbeck, *The Grapes of Wrath* (New York: The Viking Press, Inc., 1939; Bantam Books, 1970), p. 32

26.   See also Robert J. Griffin and William A. Freedman, "Machines and Animals: Pervasive Motifs in *The Grapes of Wrath,* "in Journal of English and German Philology 62 (April 1963), pp. 558-569; reprint in *A Casebook On The Grapes Of Wrath,* ed. Agnes McNeill Donohue (New York: Thomas Y. Crowell Co., 1969), pp. 219-231.

27.   The practical need of one generation becomes the art of the next. Car customizing as an art form developed in California, the state to which the dustbowl refugees drove the first 'customized' cars.

28.   For additional parallels between the prose style and subject matter of the Old Testament and *The Grapes of Wrath,* see Peter Lisca, *"The Grapes of Wrath* as Fiction," *PMLA* 62 (March 1957), pp. 296-309; reprint in *A Casebook on The Grapes of Wrath,* pp. 168-182.

29.   The last phrase is a reminder that one of the "successes" promised by the automobile was sexual success—the notion that the young man with a car has the best chance of getting the girl(s).

30.   Steinbeck's *Travels With Charley* (New York: The Viking Press, Inc., Bantam Books, 1962), written almost thirty years later, is an embarrassing parody of the best writing and passionate conviction of *The Grapes of Wrath.* At fifty-eight, Steinbeck sets out on another journey across America with no stronger motive this time than keeping his rocking chair at bay. To insure that his body is comfortably housed and insulated from the discomfort of experience, Steinbeck custom-orders a luxury camper/truck which he waggishly calls "Rocinante," after Don Quixote's broken-down nag. Along with the body, the soul and the intellect have gone soft too, and all that one gets from reading *Travels With Charley* are some *Ladies' Home Journal* style travel tips and a few scattered, unexplored ideas buried in a tedious body of material.

31.   John Dos Passos, *The Big Money: Third In The Trilogy U.S.A.* (Boston: Houghton Mifflin Company, 1933; reprint ed., 1969; Signet Classics' 1969), p. 72.

32.   According to psychiatrist Jean Rosenbaum, the automobile in America "has become the means by which man is able to actively

express his wishes for power and mastery over nature." (*Is Your Volkswagon A Sex Symbol?* [New York: Hawthorn Books, Inc., 1972; Bantam, 1973], p. 6).

33.   Peter Meinke, "Swallowing America Whole," in *New Republic*, 22 Sept. 1973, pp. 28-31.

34.   F. Scott Fitzgerald, *The Great Gatsby* (New York: Charles Scribner's Sons, 1925; reprint ed., 1953), p. 64.

4

Dreams of Possession, Nightmares of Being Possessed

When King Lear is admonished by his two daughters to give up his servants because he has no further "need" for them, he cries out:

O, reason not the need. Our basest beggars
Are in the poorest things superfluous.
Allow not nature more than nature needs,
Man's life is cheap as beast's.[1]

Lear knows that man, be he king or beggar, requires possessions in excess of basic need to confirm his identity and humanity. Ironically, of course, Lear's own experience proves otherwise. Thus it is only when he is stripped of all he has and reduced to the status of a "poor, bare, forked animal" on the heath that Lear rises to the full measure of his humanity and greatness.

As the world daily grows larger, more complex, and more impersonal, man, more than ever, seeks the security of things. To fill in the void both around and within himself, man craves possessions to give his life an identifiable and pleasing shape. Paradoxically, however, by investing inanimate objects with power and significance, the individual, like Lear, often diminishes himself. By seeking—whatever the cost—to be possessor, man often becomes, in turn, possessed. Or, as Ralph Waldo Emerson once lamented, "Things are in the saddle/ And ride mankind."[2]

When the automobile appeared in the first decade of the twentieth century, it quickly became one of the things Americans desired most. For the prestige and social status it symbolized, the mobility it afforded, the pleasure and power it gave its driver, and the sense of place and appropriation of space it allowed, the American began to consider the car not only as a prized possession but as a necessity for his well-being.

As a plaything of the rich, the car could easily be dismissed; as an indispensable part of the American life and ego, the car demands—and elicits—a more complex response. Americans have responded by handling the motor car in the same way that men, in a milieu where nature is king, have handled the mysteries and terrors of nature. In their attempts both to appropriate and understand the automobile, Americans name and anthropomorphize, ritualize and exalt their cars. They create myths and "momentary gods"[3] out of the machines that affect them most personally.

In his daily life as well as in his art, the American persists in naming his automobile. On its simplest level, a name identifies and personalizes, making familiar what once was strange. Conversely, a name may invest something mundane with an allure and mystery it would not otherwise have. One of the richest recipients of familiar or folksy names was the Model T. "Flivver," "Henry," "Henrietta," "tin can," "can opener," "sardine box," "sputter bus," "Tin Lizzie," "road louse," and "perpetual pest" are among the most amusing and best-known of these designations.[4] The origin of the nickname "Tin Lizzie" is particularly fascinating and apropos. As Hannah Campbell explains it, in the heyday of the Model T, many families employed a maid who worked at all tasks during the week but "come Sunday she strutted off to church in great dignity." These maids were often referred to as "Liz" or "Lizzie." Like its human counterpart, the Model T was also a " 'maid of all work'—sometimes used to grind fodder, churn butter, saw wood, or pull a plow in the fields—but come Sunday, she was prettied up to take the family regally to church."[5] Americans accepted their mechanical servants with the same equanimity that they had earlier accepted their human ones.

Today, car names are used to elicit different responses. Instead of reminding owners of their vehicle's grass roots practicality and necessity, car names conjure up romance, adventure, or nostalgia for a mythical past. Ford, for example, has christened some of its cars Mustangs and Pintos so that, by a kind of sympathetic magic, the individual owner can pretend he is riding a wild horse; he can imagine himself liberated from the constrictions of an urban existence and, like the young protagonist of *The Car Thief* (who also thinks of his car as a stallion), be transported for an hour or two to an illusory wild west.[6] Irrespective of their specific connotations, car names of all kinds have allowed Americans to feel closer to their cars and to make those vehicles a more integral part of the world they live in or dream about.

The anthropomorphosis or personification of the car takes the integration process one step further. Once the automobile is endowed with animate qualities, it can be treated as an extension of the self or even as an autonomous surrogate. Examples of anthropomorphized cars abound in popular culture. In the sixties, for example, millions of Americans followed the aitics of a matriarchal automobile in the TV comedy series, "My Mother, The Car," while at the movies they fell in love with Herbie, the winsome car/star of Walt Disney's *The Love Bug*. Mattel, one of the giants in the toy industry, has likewise exploited the automobile's "human" qualities in its Farb car, which features a human body in place of the traditional automobile chassis. A similar idea, raised to the level of fine art, may be found in the sculpture of Ernest Trova.

Little boys who play with little cars grow up to be big boys

The power of naming—Ford's Mustang II (Courtesy of the Ford Division, Ford Motor Company.)

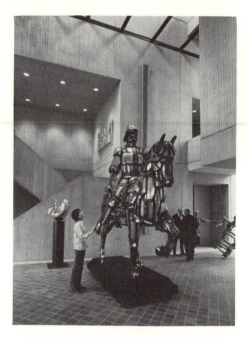

Jason Seley's *Colleoni II*, a man on horseback sculpted out of automobile bumpers. (Courtesy of Jason Seley.)

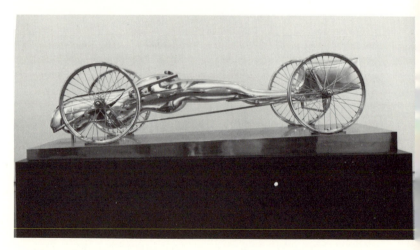

The sculpture suggests that man and his wheels are one. Ernest Trova's *Study: Falling Man (Carman)*, 1966, polished silicone bronze and enamel, measuring 21½ x 78 x 31''. (Courtesy of the Pace Gallery, New York Collection of the Whitney Museum of American Art.)

who play with big cars, often without much change in attitude. With this idea in mind, perhaps, Fred Muir has written a new kind of practical car manual. In his introduction to *How To Keep Your VW Alive*, Muir says, quite seriously: "Your car is constantly telling your senses where it's at. I don't speak 'donkey,' but I am fairly conversant in 'vw' and will help you learn the basic vocabulary of this language so your Bus, Bug, or Ghia can become an extension of your own sensory equipment." Muir concludes his introduction with the following advice: "Talk to the car, then shut up and listen. Feel with your car; use all of your receptive senses and when you find out what it needs, seek the operation out and perform it with love. The type of life your car contains differs from yours by time scale, logic level, and conceptual anomalies, but it is 'life' none the less. Its Karma depends on your desire to make and keep it . . . ALIVE!"[7]

If Muir can sell a practical car manual with such a humanizing, anthropomorphic approach, it is small wonder that many car mechanics today sport white frock coats disquietingly similar to those worn by physicians, that there are growing numbers of automotive diagnostic centers (Mayo Clinics for cars), and that a new auto body shop in Cleveland is not called that at all but is designated a "Car-Aid Center." With flowers, shrubs, and picket fence outside and a reception area inside complete with upholstered chairs and coffee for its often distraught clients, "Car-Aid" is truly an out-patient clinic for man's four-wheeled extensions.[8] The anthropomorphosis of the car is not relegated to popular culture and body shops alone; serious writers and observers of the American scene have also given the car human atrributes and gone on to explore their ramifications for man. Sociologist Kenneth Schneider, for example, talks about the car as if it (she?) were a demanding, destructive mistress, tyrannizing man and his habitat.[9] As we have seen in the novels of Hawkes, Faulkner, and Fitzgerald, cars function as extensions of the human protagonists; in the work of other artists, the car functions as a person in its own right, eliciting the same emotional reactions and experiences that normally only a human relationship would provide.

In his delightful poem, "XIX," e. e. cummings equates driving his brand-new car to making it with a virgin:

i was

careful of her and (having
thoroughly oiled the universal
joint tested my gas felt of
her radiator made sure her springs were O.
K.) i went right to it[10]

The generous use of the feminine possessive establishes the car's "human" role in the lovemaking. Meanwhile, the halting approach of the neophyte driver to his virginal mistress is reinforced by the varied movement and often halting rhythm (poeticus interruptus!) of the poem. When the driver's first overardent attempt to get started fails, he slows down both his movement and that of the verse. When everything is finally working well, the lines also flow more smoothly:

oh and her gears being in
A 1 shape passed
from low through
second-in-to-high like
greasedlightning) just as we turned the corner
          of Divinity

avenue i touched the accelerator and give

her the juice, good

The poem ends on a "divine" note of union as the now more self-assured driver takes control, bringing his trembling mistress to a

:dead
stand—
;still)

Tangential to his amusing play on sexually suggestive words and rhythms, cummings is saying something about the car as a particular kind of possession. In certain primitive societies, the concept of ownership began with the male's ownership of the woman.[11] In contemporary democratic societies, complete appropriation is associated with things rather than people, yet vestiges of primitive thinking survive in modern man's regarding his mechanical possessions as female. Airplanes, boats, and, of course, cars are "female." American males lavish affection, attention, and money on their cars, sometimes more than on their flesh-and-blood females. "The American," William Faulkner once remarked cynically, "really loves nothing but his automobile."[12] Similarly, cummings indicates in "XIX" that his car is both female and cherished possession; therefore his driving of that car is, literally and figuratively, an act of love.

In his macabre novel *V.*, Thomas Pynchon reverses the traditional male/car relationship spoofed by cummings. In *V.* it is a female, Rachel Owlglass, who finds the object of her affections not in any male that she meets but in her little "inanimate" MG. Rachel's world is one of "objects coveted and valued" and at its apex is the car, to which she talks "nothing but MG-words." Benny Profane comes upon Rachel one night as she is washing and talking to her car:

"You beautiful stud," he heard her say, "I love to touch you." Wha, he thought. "Do you know what I feel when we're out on the road? Alone, just us?" She was running the sponge caressingly over its front bumper. "Your funny responses, darling, that I know so well. The way your brakes pull a little to the left, the way you start to shudder around 5000 rpm when you're excited. And you burn oil when you're mad at me, don't you? I know. . . . We'll always be together," running a chamois over the hood, "and you needn't worry about that black Buick we passed on the road today. Ugh: fat, greasy Mafia car. I expected to see a body come flying out the back door, didn't you? Besides, you're so angular and proper-English and

tweedy—and oh, so Ivy that I couldn't ever leave you,
dear."13

Pynchon's comic tour-de-force provides a brilliant and
devastating commentary on the American attachment to
objects, in this case, Rachel's erotic love for her car. Benny, as
the voice of reason ("Wha, he thought"), is rendered speechless
by this irrational attraction of a warm and loving young woman
to an inanimate thing. He watches dumbfounded as Rachel
makes sexual overtures to her car; she "caresses," "fondles,"
and "touches" its phallic protuberances (hood, front bumper,
gearshift). She even talks to it, asking questions and praising it
as she would a diffident human lover. By this time it occurs to
Profane that he might be sick, not because the object of her
affections is what it is, but because "public displays of senti-
ment often affected him in this way." As casually as Rachel,
who seems otherwise sane, accepts the car as her lover, Benny
the protester acquiesces to being shut out by an MG.

What Pynchon is trying to say in this vignette, as elsewhere
in *V.*, is that in humanizing objects, people tend to dehumanize
themselves. When a beautiful young woman loves only her MG
and talks to it in MG words, then communication between
human beings has been supplanted by a new form of dialogue in
which people talk and respond only to things. More unsettling
still, the blurring of distinctions between animate and inanimate results in the treatment of human beings as if they too
were objects. Hitler, Eichmann, and Mengele were archmas-
ters of this technique: "remember," asks Profane, "the photographs of Auschwitz? Thousands of Jewish corpses, stacked up
like those poor car-bodies in a junked car lot" (p. 275). For e. e.
cummings, love affair between owner and car is fodder for
ribald good humor; for Pynchon, it is an occasion for unsettling
black comedy.

If an individual is capable of treating the automobile as a
surrogate human, it is but one short, inevitable step further to
treat that car as a surrogate god. Cassirer says that as soon as
man employs a tool, he views it "not as a mere artifact of which
he is the recognized maker, but as a Being in its own right,

endowed with powers of its own. Instead of being governed by his will, it becomes a god or daemon on whose will he depends—to which he feels himself subjected, and which he adores with the rites of a religious cult."[14] Although Cassirer is speaking of primitive cultures, this attitude toward tools survives today.

Certainly one of the most graphic examples of twentieth-century tool-worship is the American attitude toward the automobile. Andrew Greeley makes explicit the connection between mythico-religious thinking and American automania when he says:

> one need merely visit the annual automobile show to realize that it is a highly ritualized religious performance. The colors, the lights, the music, the awe of the worshippers, the presence of temple priestesses (fashion models), the pomp and splendor, the lavish waste of money, the thronging crowds—all these would represent in any other culture a clearly liturgical service. . . . The cult of the sacred car has its adepts and its initiati. No gnostic more eagerly awaited a revelation from an oracle than does an automobile worshipper await the first rumors about the new models. It is at this time of the annual seasonal cycle that the high priests of the cult—the auto dealers—take on a new importance as an anxious public eagerly expects the coming of a new form of salvation."[15]

Just as the annual automobile show is a "highly ritualized religious performance," so the average American has made his own personal car the object of certain ritual acts: with undeviating regularity he washes it, polishes it, and uses it for the family's Sunday outing. Herman Mack, the protagonist of Harry Crews' novel, *Car*, takes this trend further by making the automobile the focus of ritual reenactments of important and even sacred moments in human life. As the "mad dreamer" of the car-crushing Mack family, Herman dreams up "Car Display: Your History On Parade," a historical retrospective enacted through cars. "Everything that's happened in this god-

dam country in the last fifty years," explains Herman, "has
happened in, on, around, with, or near a car." So Herman finds
a representative car for each year between 1920 and 1970 and
invites people to return to "the scene of the crime." Herman's
billboard reads, "SEE THE CAR IT HAPPENED IN—THE EVENT THAT
CHANGED YOUR LIFE." And the people come: "to relive the love
affair, the accident, that first car, that last car, the time the tire
went flat, the time he ran out of gas, the time he *said* he ran out
of gas, the place where Junior was conceived ('You had your
foot braced against the door handle, honey. Remember?')."[16]

Placed within the context of American life, Herman's
scheme to rediscover and reenact individual experience
through facsimile cars is not altogether absurd. Because Americans spend a great deal of time in their cars—often using them
as surrogate homes, offices, and bedrooms—the automobile is,
inevitably, the scene of many important events. Furthermore,
as we have seen in *The Grapes of Wrath*, the sacred places of
one's life, like almost all structures outliving their utility or
modernity in America, become victims of the bulldozer. Often,
all that is left to sustain the imagination or express the unity of
personal life is what one can salvage from an attic or a wrecked
car lot. Therefore it is in objects—and particularly in the automobile—that the rootless American can pay tribute (i.e., ritually return) to some of the central occurrences in his life.
Herman intuitively understands Americans' vague longings for
a sense of place and orientation in their lives, and he recognizes
his cars' value in assuaging those longings.

When family pressures force Herman to close down "Car
Display," he comes up with the even wilder scheme to EAT a
car. The night before the widely publicized extravaganza of
eating begins, Herman experiences an epiphany. Lying out-
stretched on the Ford Maverick provided for his consumption,
Herman "solemnly opened his mouth as though about to take
upon his tongue a sacrament, but instead his pink lolling tongue
lapped out of his mouth and touched metal, touched the hood
of the Maverick car. It was clean and cold and he felt himself
tighten around his stomach. He longed to have it in his mouth.

To feel it in his throat. To hold it in his stomach. It would amaze the world" (pp. 54-55).

Although the author deliberately and amusingly confuses a sacred with a sexual act, Herman's touching the car with his tongue is, for him, a purely religious experience. In this moment, the secular ritual associated with "Car Display" is transformed into the private religious ritual of direct communion with his motorized god. As a disciple who partakes of painted metal sacraments, however, Herman is doomed to pain and suffering. At first he has nightmares about being a car-/Christ himself, whose immortality resides in numerous junkyards ready to yield up spare parts, to "replace everything with all things until he was nobody because he was everybody" (p. 79). After the psychic pain, the physical pain attached to eating and passing begins. Herman "hurt in a long devious line starting at his mouth and running down his throat through long curling intestines and ending at his anus. And it hurt all the worse because he still loved the car" (p. 115).

Although the novel ends weakly with Herman simply giving up the Maverick for Margo, a hotel whore with a heart of gold, the reader may draw his own inferences from this bizarre parable. He realizes that while Herman may conceive of the car as an abstract deity, the Ford's physical reality (e.g., the indigestibility of its parts) takes priority. Despite the zealous devotion of its worshipper, the car as metal and glass and vinyl object proves to be a more formidable and recalcitrant force than the car as religious incarnation. By attempting to deify and then consume what was simply meant to be driven, Herman demeans himself and suffers great mental and physical anguish as well. Whereas Herman's goal is to devour (i.e., literally possess) the car, the car more nearly succeeds in devouring him.

Flannery O'Connor, a better and more important writer than Crews, has also explored man's private devotion to the car. The main plot of her novel *Wise Blood* deals with Hazel Motes who, upon completing four years in the army, sets out to find a place for himself in the big city. Dissatisfied with his initial "home" in the house of an aging prostitute, Motes decides to buy a car. He spends fifty dollars on a "high, rat-colored" broken-down old Essex and tells the dealer as he prepares to drive away, "I wanted this car mostly to be a house for me; I ain't got any place to be."[17] Soon it becomes apparent that Motes' sense of place is more than merely physical. Despite his rantings to the contrary, he also wants to find a spiritual home for himself, and the car offers a perfect solution. It becomes a pulpit from which the deracinated Motes can preach his philosophy of "The Church Without Christ." With biting wit, O'Connor notes that even the windshield wipers on the Essex "made a great clatter like two idiots clapping in church" (p. 44). Although the belligerent Motes attracts no one to his place of worship except an unscrupulous "prophet" who sees in him an easy source of money, the car, like a church, gives him refuge from the ugliness and evil around him. That was "the advantage of having a car—of having something that moves fast, in privacy, to the place you wanted to be" (p. 101). In Hazel's mind, the Essex also serves as a source of redemption. "No one with a good car needs to be justified," he insists (p. 64). The irony here, as elsewhere, is doublefold. Motes' sputtering, coughing, fifty-dollar junker is anything but a good car, and if O'Connor is to be taken at her word, Christ, not some mechanical surrogate serving as a pulpit for denying Him, is the only justification for living or dying.[18]

In addition to providing Hazel Motes with ordination (he becomes a preacher on the hood of the Essex) and redemption, the car also performs godlike vengeance. The Essex punishes its impersonator, another rat-colored car, by forcing it off the road and running over its driver, the false prophet, Solace Layfield. Shortly before Motes' car meets its death at the hands of a nonbelieving policeman who pushes it over an embankment, the Essex performs its final religious office: on its way to a new city (the New Jerusalem?), the car leaves "little bead-chains of water and oil and gas on the road" (p. 112). After the Essex is martyred, its only true disciple has no alternative but to follow the same course. With a quiet sense of purpose and acceptance he has never known before, Motes blinds himself.

Car as church: life copies art of *Wise Blood*. Reverend Robert Schuller delivers a sermon to parishioners in what is thought to be the nation's first drive-in church at Garden Grove, California. He calls the church "a 22-acre shopping center for Jesus Christ" (1972). (Used with permission of Wide World Photos, Inc.)

All his life there has been a haze or mote in his eye; now, in blindness, he thinks he sees the inner light.

In *Wise Blood*, the car functions in the double role of possession and possessor. Initially, and on the most literal level, the Essex is Hazel Motes' possession which he uses as home, pulpit, and mode of transportation. As the story progresses, however, the car becomes Hazel Motes' symbolic possessor—his spiritual Father and God. Whereas Motes begins by paying money for the car (the initial act of appropriation), he ends by paying obeisance to it. Finally, it is not the physical presence of the Essex that matters, because the car has long been demolished, but its spiritual effect on Motes, who follows its path to a similar and (one can't help feeling) gratuitous martyrdom at the hands of the police.

As in *Wise Blood*, O'Connor's short story, "The Life You Save May Be Your Own," also expresses ambivalence about the car as surrogate god and redeemer. The protagonist of "The Life You Save" is Tom Shiftlet, a one-armed carpenter with a mechanical bent. Shiftlet appears at Lucynell Crater's farm one day, his figure forming "a crooked cross" against the sky. [19] The carpenter's discerning eye quickly passes over the rapacious Mrs. Crater and her grown retarded daughter, Lucy, and lights upon the one thing that holds any interest for him, a rusted old automobile standing in a shed. Without revealing his intentions, Shiftlet offers to fix up the Crater "plantation" in return for food and a makeshift bed in back of the car. After a week of proving himself around the farm, Shiftlet starts to work on the real object of his devotion, the car. Finally, "with a volley of blasts it emerged from the shed, moving in a fierce and stately way. Mr. Shiftlet was in the driver's seat, sitting very erect. He had an expression of serious modesty on his face as if he had just raised the dead" (pp. 165-166).

The life this mechanical Christ saves is not that of the poor (Mrs. Crater) or the simple (her daughter) but that of the car. By extension, Shiftlet attempts to save his own life as well. The carpenter makes the connection when he says to Mrs. Crater, "the body, lady, is like a house. It don't go anywhere; but the spirit, lady, is like a automobile: always on the move, always"

(p. 166). A little later he adds, "a man's spirit means more to him than anything else" (p. 167). Soon Shiftlet acts out the meaning of his ironic parables. Once Mrs. Crater consents to financing a wedding trip by car, Shiftlet marries her retarded daughter. With money in his pocket and gas in the tank, the new bridegroom soon abandons his human cargo at a nearby diner and races in his "spirit" toward Mobile.

The title of this beautifully executed short story sets the ambivalent tone for the whole piece. "The life you save may be your own" is a common sign on roads and highways; it is the explanation and justification for the preceding admonition to "drive carefully." The author, however, sees this seemingly innocuous appeal to one's instinct for self-preservation as a pervasive and reprehensible fact of modern life. Everyone in the story, except the counterboy who is moved by the innocently sleeping figure of Lucynell, is out for himself. Shiftlet wants a car. Mrs. Crater is "ravenous" for a son-in-law. The young hitchhiker whom Shiftlet picks up wants to get away from home and his "flea bag" mother. In this atmosphere of greed to possess what one wants and to mercilessly cast off what one doesn't want, an old rusted car and a tramp who isn't even a complete man are the only Christ figures that deserve to appear.

Yet for all her cynicism, O'Connor is not without some hope for redemption and change. In the closing paragraphs, Shiftlet himself undergoes a crisis of conscience. He is "more depressed than ever" after he abandons his bride and is shocked by a hitchhiker's brutal acknowledgment of their hatred for what, in a Christian world, both should love (mother, wife). Conscious now of his own "rottenness" and that of the world around him, Shiftlet implores the true Christ to save him. "'Oh Lord!' he prayed. 'Break forth and wash the slime from this earth.'" As if in answer to his prayers, the thunder sounds and "fantastic raindrops" begin to fall (p. 170).

In "The Life You Save," the car functions in Manichean ways. During the early part of the story, the car is a nascent devil or tempter, beguiling Shiftlet into making elaborate schemes for its resurrection and possession. But in O'Connor's

universe, God even speaks through the devil; hence, it is while
he is in the car that Shiftlet first experiences a twinge of
Christian remorse for his sins and takes the initial step of
reconciling himself to his true Redeemer. With deliberate
ambiguity, however, O'Connor chooses as her last image the
picture of Shiftlet racing the galloping shower into Mobile.
While the rain may serve to cleanse this maimed Christ of his
sins, the destination of Mobile (a name which suggest cars)
implies that more false gods await Shiftlet, threatening again to
blunt his Christian purpose.

Whereas O'Connor prefers to leave her tale of Shiftlet, his
car, and his redemption open-ended, Norman Mailer uses an
automobile to close the circle on his technical, literary, and
philosophical journey to the moon. In the last chapter of *Of A
Fire On The Moon*, his extraordinary book on the Apollo 11
flight, Mailer describes the burial of an old Ford in Provincetown. It is at the end of the summer during which man first
went to the moon, walked on it, and brought a piece of it back.
If a piece of the moon could be salvaged from that summer,
Mailer's earth-bound marriage of seven years could not. "Mar-
riages," he says, referring to his own and those of four neigh-
bors, "were breaking up as fast as tires blowing in a long race."[20]
By Labor Day, what is pervasive is a sense of an ending; an end
to summer, to love, to the fantastic, almost incomprehensible
voyage to the moon. To commemorate these endings, Mailer
and his friends attend still another kind of ending, the death
and ritual burial of their neighbor's Ford.

Though it is conceived in playfulness and executed with
mock solemnity and pomposity, the act of burial speaks symbolically of the strong bond between man and his possessions.
Sartre says that the "recognition that it is impossible to *possess*
an object involves . . . a violent urge to destroy it. Destruction
realizes appropriation perhaps more keenly than creation does,
for the object destroyed is no longer there to show itself
impenetrable."[21] The wearing out of the car (at its purchase, the
owners request that the vehicle "manage to survive" only
through part of September) and its subsequent burial and
transformation are forms of destruction. "Something in the

mood of summer," Mailer writes (is it the need to destroy? or to create?) "brought every neighbor in for the burial" (p. 404).

Not content to dispose of the car in any ordinary way, Mailer and his friends give the Ford the panoply of a pagan/Christian "Burial By The Sea."[22] A proper grave is dug, neighboring poets function as sacramental officers, and a boy wearing the black robes of a Byzantine priest reads "somber verses from Virgil, the Latin passing like a wash of coagulants over the car" (p. 404). In addition to these formalized last rites, personal eulogies are read. Final confirmation of the car's "humanness" comes from the labored respiration of the vehicle itself when a boy reaches into the grave and flicks on the windshield wipers. " 'My God, it's not dead yet' said a voice. But as if in a throe of its last effluents, the washers began to spurt a final lymph" (p. 405).

If the car is human in its own right, it is also an extension of its owners and mourners. As every man buries something of himself that Labor Day—his love affair with the moon (divested now of her ancient mystery and attraction), his marriage, his summer—he symbolizes that loss in the burial of the Ford. This car, "this buried friend," provides the occasion for heroic poems, for drunkenness, and for the mourning of other losses still more painful. Like the skull of poor Yorick to which Mailer compares it (p. 406), the burial of the car is at once personal and absurd, solemn and funny.

Once the Ford is buried, its hood facing the sky, the children ritually adorn it as befits a god or totem. Then, in an act parallel to Mailer's act of writing an original, creative book about the moon shot, Kearney, the master of the burial rites, applies a fiery torch and transforms the exposed portion of the car into a work of art. With Kafkaesque instinct, he makes the Ford into a giant insect. The funeral ends in "an artifact for the summer of the moon in the East End of Provincetown . . . *Metamorphosis*, titled by Kearney, a massive Yorick of half a Ford standing twelve feet high, first machine to die with burial in the land of the Pilgrims and the cod" (p. 407). The return of the car to the earth—and specifically the earth of Provincetown, where

America first began—is Mailer's ritual celebration not only of the Ford, America's prototypical car, but of that primary American possession, the land. The appropriated place—one's car—is returned to the communal place of origin; man's latest love is returned to the locus of his first love. Mythically and historically, the sense of possession comes full circle.

In addition to rounding out his sense of history, Mailer's burial of the Ford solves certain problems in the book itself. About a decade before the moon shot, Hugh Kenner wrote that "it is normal for territories the imagination has once pioneered to be occupied at last by hardware";[23] in *Of A Fire On The Moon,* Mailer tries to reverse the trend by taking the hardware and making of it a territory for the imagination. Mailer understands that if the American imagination is to be captured by an event, it must be capable somehow of assimilating that event within the realm of its own experience. Art often provides the necessary assimilation process. But when the scope of the event becomes almost more than human in dimension, as the moon shot did, art is often not enough; despite Mailer's impressive efforts, the reader may not be able to make the imaginative leap of faith required of him to absorb the experience. Sensing his reader's problem—as well as his own—in coming to grips with the miraculous and, in many ways, terrifying technological feat of putting a man on the moon, Mailer feels the need to get back to a technology more compatible with the human psyche. Hence he returns, at the end, to the one machine still capable of being romanticized, humanized, and deified by the human imagination; he returns to the car and the numerous rites of appropriation accompanying its burial by the sea.

What Mailer does for the theme of car-as-possession in *Of A Fire On The Moon,* Claes Oldenburg does in the plastic arts: he destroys the original form of the automobile in order to reshape or repossess it again on his own terms. Oldenburg's interest in technology dates back to his early drawings of plants metamorphosed into machines; from that point, it was only a matter of time before Oldenburg began to focus on the automobile in particular. During his stay in Los Angeles (the only city in the world with more cars than people), Oldenburg's fascination with the car grew. There, in 1963, he organized and staged *Autobodys*, a form of drive-in happening in which the spectators took part by providing illumination for the events with their cars' headlights.[24] In 1965, the artist began work on a much larger and more permanent project, *The Airflow. The Airflow* consisted of "soft machines" (the prototype for his whole series of soft machines) and, later, molded plastic multiples. All of these works are based on Oldenburg's studies of the Chrysler Airflow engine, designed in 1935 by his father's good friend, the sculptor and filmmaker Carl Breer.

An articulate spokesman for his own art and aesthetics, Oldenburg writes in his journals about the car as artistic motif. On a symbolic level, the artist sees the car as an icon or a way to make meaning out of the age. Drawing upon the same image as the Italian Futurists (the first group of artists to depict the automobile in their art), Oldenburg wants the car to be for Americans what the Winged Victory of Samothrace was for the Greeks. There is a direct parallel between the Airflow and the Winged Victory because the Airflow design, according to Breer, was based on a study of birds in flight. In yet another Futurist vein, Oldenburg sees man in his car as a kind of modern centaur, a mythical revitalization of that ancient race, half human, half wild animal, translated in terms of a superman behind the wheel. Oldenburg also conceives of the car as an "environment," "a gallery, a store—with many objects in it."[25] Within the bounds of this manufactured environment, man finds a sense of space and enjoys his mastery of it.

Most important—and most like Mailer—Oldenburg considers the car as man's double (in Swedish, "Karl" means both "car" and "guy").[26] It is, he says, in terms reminiscent of John Hawkes, man's shell or second skin. "My car," he writes elsewhere in his notebook, "is probably the deepest most natural subject I've had."[27] Because he considers the car as a visual metaphor or surrogate for the human body, Oldenburg studied the car as a student of anatomy studies the human form. Using detailed drawings and photographs, he analyzed and recreated the "car as body, flayed, as in an anatomical chart. Cloth as sheet of tissue, rope as muscle."[28] The irony of the

Claes Oldenburg's *Soft Chrysler Airflow #2*, 1965. Muslin stenciled and stuffed with kapok, 23″ long, private collection. (Courtesy of Sidney Janis Gallery, New York; photo by Geoffrey Clements.)

Claes Oldenburg's *Soft Engine. Airflow Model #6*, 1966. Stenciled canvas, wood, kapok, 54 x 72 x 18″. Collection of Dr. Hubert Peeters, Bruges. (Courtesy of Sidney Janis Gallery, New York; photo by Geoffrey Clements.)

Claes Oldenburg's *Profile of Chrysler Airflow*, 1968-69. Molded polyurethane over two-color, hand-printed lithograph, 32½ x 64½''. (Courtesy of Progressive Corporation, Cleveland, Ohio; photo by Jon Lewis.)

The Keystone Kops: anarchy in control. (Used with permission of Culver Pictures.) Keystone Kops: "A troupe of slapstick comedians . . . who from 1912-1920 made innumerable violent comedies full of wild chases and trick effects." [Leslie Halliwell, *The Filmgoer's Companion*, 3rd ed. (New York: Hill & Wang, 1965, 1970.)]

artist's precise anatomical investigations is that he transforms his subject matter into its tactile and physical opposite, most of the *Airflow* pieces being made of stencilled canvas filled with kapok. In this deliberate reversal from hard to soft forms, Oldenburg "makes technology . . . vulnerable."[29] Like Kearnry's transformation of the car into an insect, the creation and metamorphosis of the Airflow into a harmless force represents Oldenburg's way of possessing and controlling a potentially destructive god of automobiles. A decade earlier, Oldenburg's good friend and artistic inspiration, Jackson Pollock, had been killed in an automobile accident; now Oldenburg was working on an automobile rendered powerless to kill or maim. The work of art was conceived in part, then, as a "magic talisman that would protect the artist himself from destruction."[30] By appropriating the car as his artistic milieu, by seeing it as an icon for the age, an extension of the self and a surrogate human and god, Oldenburg's art, like Mailer's, represents multiple facets of possession. Yet the rationale behind artistic possession differs markedly for the two artists. For Mailer, getting back to earth after the moon shot, the Ford represents a return to a more comprehensible and controllable reality; for Oldenburg, the Chrysler Airflow represents an escape from the real-life cars he cannot control.

Except, perhaps, for artistic creation, the various acts of naming, anthropomorphizing, ritualizing, and deifying the car are often as elusive in their end result as the dream of possession that begot them. For example, despite its nominal associations with free-spirited animality, the Mustang is as likely to get bogged down in traffic as a car with a less suggestive name; and for all its surface sex appeal or incipient "humanity," the car cannot satisfactorily replace more traditional human relationships. More pertinent still, to elevate a car to the status of human or god is to court, as in the work of Pynchon, Crews, and O'Connor, a dangerous reversal of roles between possessor and possession.

Analyzing this situation from a sociological viewpoint, Kenneth Schneider writes that after 1912, as the automobile was said to have

> attained an "age of maturity" . . . the worm began to turn. Words changed. Facts changed. Ever so subtly Americans ceased to judge the motor car and the motor car began to judge America. Subject and object had switched, not only in grammar. So had means and ends. By 1920 it was common to use such phrases as the "faith of motor-car makers in the future buying power of the nation."[31]

Schneider goes on to point out some of the deleterious effects of this reversal of roles. He says that "to the extent that our civilization becomes dependent upon the automobile we reduce ourselves and our character of mind to a new species of being, a society of invertebrates as clumsy as a convention of turtles. The way we honor our new shells makes one wonder whether we have an atavistic urge to junk our whole mammalian inheritance" (p. 71). Elsewhere, Schneider implies that rather than having simply junked our "mammalian inheritance," we have transferred it to our cars. Hence, gas stations, garages, used-car lots, new-car dealers, and junkyards are "the urban spaces devoted to delivering newborn cars, feeding and nursing them, holding them for readoption, and burying them" (p. 61). The irony is that as the car becomes increasingly organic in terms of its demands and constant needs, man and his environment grow increasingly inorganic and impotent. Herman Mack realizes this the first time a terrible accident occurs on a new six-lane expressway built against the wishes of the neighboring people: like a latter-day Prufrock beset by powerlessness and rage, he cries out: "I only know that I refuse to have my life measured out in cars. . . . Goddam cars are measuring *me*! *Me*! Don't you see we're on the wrong end."[32]

Americans have also found themselves "on the wrong end" when the cars in which they have invested such power seem to use that power in gratuitously destructive ways. In the early years of the automobile, when the six-lane highway existed only in the realm of science fiction, the theme of the machine out of control was mainly the province of the filmmaker, his acrobatic actors, and his trick photography camera man. According to novelist and film critic James Agee, the consummate master of "giving inanimate objects a mischievous life of their own" and then setting them free to wreak chaos was Mack Sennett. A staple of Sennett's Keystone Kop films, for example, was the chase. As Agee describes it, toward the end of almost every Sennett comedy, "a chase (usually called the 'rally') built up such a majestic trajectory of pure anarchic motion that bathing girls, cops, comics, dogs, cats, babies, automobiles, locomotives, innocent bystanders, sometimes what seemed like a whole city, an entire civilization, were hauled along head over heels in the wake of that energy like dry leaves following an express train."[33]

The important part of Agee's description here is his simile, "like dry leaves following an express train." It is an image that, while suggesting the exhilarating effect of motion, makes that motion devoid of terror or disaster. By a kind of fantastic legerdemain unique to the movies, the anarchy that is loosed upon the world ends before the final frame without any real mishaps. For the moviegoer, the excitement of the Sennett chase resides in the potential for disaster; the comforting reassurance is that that potential will never be realized. Once, Agee points out, "a low-comedy auto got out of control and killed the cameraman, but he was not visible in the shot, which was thrilling and undamaged; the audience never knew the difference."[34]

Whereas disaster in a movie can be relegated to the cutting room floor, it is not so easily disposed of offscreen. No one understood this better than Agee himself who, at the same time as he was writing about the comic effects of runaway cars, was also working on a different version of that phenomenon in his largely autobiographical novel, *A Death In The Family.*[35] While stylistically there is a direct parallel between the "vision" of the silent movie camera and the "vision" of the mature narrative voice in *A Death In The Family*, thematically the parallel becomes tragically inverted.[36] In the movies, the multiple collisions are sheer fantasy; in the novel, the lone car crash is all too real, as is the disaster that follows in its unmajestic wake.

Agee's plot spans a seventy-two hour period in the lives of the Follet family. In the early hours of a May morning, Jay and Mary Follet are awakened by an urgent phone call from Jay's younger brother, Ralph. Their father appears to be dying; would Jay come as soon as possible? Jay dresses, eats hurriedly, and then begins the long solitary drive to his parents' farm. Finding that Ralph (probably drunk at the time) has exaggerated about his father's condition, Jay starts the drive home again the next evening. At 10 P.M. Mary Follet gets a phone call; Jay has met with a terrible accident. During the final stretch of that fast drive, a cotter pin fell out, causing the steering mechanism to fail; the automobile veered out of control and overturned. Jay was killed instantly.

As the title indicates, the whole structure and texture of the novel revolves around the fatal automobile crash. The car itself has always played an important and ambivalent role in the Follets' lives. Stylistically, Agee treats the ambivalence to cars—and machines in general—in terms of noise and silences. In "Knoxville: Summer, 1915," the prefatory essay to *A Death In The Family*, silences and soft, comforting sounds—hoses spraying lawns, crickets, locusts, the low voices of adults after dinner—are associated with the narrator's tranquil memories of childhood.[37] Yet even in this pastoral overture there is the harsh, cacophanous note of a street car "raising its iron moan; stopping, belling and starting; stertorous" (p. 14).

The single discordant note in "Knoxville: Summer, 1915" takes on more ominous significance in the fully orchestrated reminiscence that is *A Death In The Family*. The low-key, touching scene between Jay and Mary before Jay leaves, for example, ends on the jarring notes of a car pulling out of the driveway:

Uhgh—hy uh yu hy why uhy uh: wheek-uh-wheek-uh: *Ughh*—hy wh yuh: wheek: (pp. 46-47)

For a page and a half, Agee poetically diagrams the full
cacophony of that doomed departure. Almost as if it sensed the
impending tragedy, the car acts pained and anguished at being
roused: "like a hideous, horribly constipated great brute of a
beast: like a lunatic sobbing: like a mouse being tortured" (p.
46). But Jay refuses to be intimidated and soon, under his
coaxing, "the engine sounded different, a smooth, easy drone;
. . . the auto bored through the center of the darkness of the
universe; its poring shafts of light, like an insect's antennae,
feeling into distinctness every relevant small obstacle and ease
of passage, and very little else" (p. 49).

The same movement from strident noise, to barely audible
comforting sound, to silence, is picked up again in the flashback
that follows, in the second section dealing with Jay's death, and
finally at the novel's close. The flashback, filtered in part
through young Rufus Follet's consciousness, takes the sounds
from "Knoxville: Summer, 1915" and transposes them into a
jarring, atonal key. Unable to sleep, Rufus listens to the summer night: "all the air vibrated like a fading bell with the latest
exhausted screaming of locusts. Couplings clashed and con-
joined; a switch engine breathed heavily. An auto engine bore
beyond the edge of audibility the furious expletives of its
incompetence" (p. 81). Panicked by these noises (only a few are
listed here) and by unanswered questions about his own identity, Rufus screams out for his father. Jay comes into the room
and kneels, as in a posture of prayer, before the child's crib.
Then kindly, masterfully, as earlier in the book he had tamed
his automobile, Jay succeeds in comforting the distraught child
by quietly talking and singing to him.

In section two, the careful patterning of the reader's
response to noise and quiet is abruptly shattered—as are Jay's
assumptions about the car he possesses and allegedly controls.
Whereas earlier the cessation of noise marked the resumption
of tranquillity, the opposite is true in the accident scene. The
closest witness to the event describes how "all of a sudden . . .
he heard a perfectly terrifying noise, just a second or two, and
then dead silence" (p. 153). In that silence, Jay Follet's life
abruptly and gratuitously is snuffed out.

The symphony of sounds and silences is concluded in the novel's last pages as Uncle Andrew describes Jay's burial to young Rufus, who has not been allowed to attend. Uncle Andrew relates how "a perfectly magnificent butterfly settled on the—coffin, just rested there, right over the breast, and stayed there, just barely making his wings breathe, like a heart" (p. 314). Then, as suddenly as it had alighted, the butterfly flew away. This "miraculous creature" represents both the antithesis and the reincarnation of the vehicle that has brought the family to this juncture in the first place. In its delicate, mute beauty, the butterfly stands in sharp contrast to the ponderous, noisy machine that disturbed the silence of a summer night and the unity of a loving family; the old Tin Lizzie has eclipsed life and the butterfly, symbolically, has opened it up again. In a more subtle sense, however, the butterfly is simply the natural prototype for the car which, under Jay's mastery, was also like a brilliant insect, responding to and illuminating the physical contours of the night. The tragedy, in fact, lies in the parallel course both butterfly and car take. Just as the butterfly suddenly and wantonly flies away, so the car, likewise defiant of human mastery and will, flies out of control.

On still another thematic level, the car serves to crystallize the fragile, often difficult relationships that exist within the family. Jay's younger brother Ralph, insecure about his own self-image, takes solace in owning a Chalmers, "a better class of auto and a more expensive one," he boasts, than Jay's Tin Lizzie. Jay, insular by nature and unconcerned about status, is happiest when driving alone and fast. Mary, who is more emotional and superstitious than her husband, feels anxious and even threatened by Jay's speeding. Finally, to six-year-old Rufus Follet, the car is a central image around which his concept of family develops. In a flashback, Rufus remembers how, on a visit to his great-great-grandmother one Sunday, his father "guided the auto so very carefully across the deep ruts in the road . . . that they were hardly joggled at all, and his mother commented on how very nicely and carefully his father always drove when he didn't just forget and go too fast, and his father blushed" (p. 215). On that same memorable trip, Uncle Ralph had insisted on showing the way and, typically, had gotten everyone lost. The allusions to Jay's speeding, Mary's uneasiness, Ralph's insistent blundering, and, above all, to Rufus' blind trust in his elders' protectiveness and love set the stage for the tragic drama to be played out.

The exact cause of Jay's death—a tiny blow to the end of the chin—was, as the family learns later, "a chance in a million" (p. 163). The irony of that statistic, like the ironic reversal of assumptions about the car as possession and man as its possessor, reverberates through the remainder of the book. Agee implies that despite man's proprietary attitude toward his automobile, the car may have a life or, in the Follets' case, a death force that ultmately eludes appropriation. Thus, despite Jay's belief that he can master his machine, there is always the possibility, even one in a million, of the automobile's careening out of control. Conversely, Agee suggests, to deny the car a determinism of its own is to implicate the man whose possession it is; in this case, the car as flawed and fallible agent is only an extension of the driver himself. "Good ole whiskey" (p. 257), one of the school boys taunts Rufus, caused the accident; "Ole Tin Lizzie" (pp. 256, 257), says another, got Jay Follet killed. The parallel phrasing suggests two variations on the same theme: under certain circumstances, man cannot control himself or his car, and in Thomas Hardy-like world where neither God nor anyone else controls or cares, tragedy is left to its own devices.

In this complex novel, the car operates on both a literal and symbolic level. As an imperfect machine, driven by a man whose own self-mastery at the time was seriously open to question, the car precipitates an accident that kills its owner and profoundly alters and saddens the Follet family. On a symbolic level, the car is a catalyst, setting in motion wanton destruction and remaining itself unscathed, save for a dropped cotter pin. Mary's father sums up the situation in a quotation from *King Lear*: "as flies to wanton boys are we to the gods; they kill us for their sport" (p. 163). Counterbalancing the impetus to destroy, however, the car accident is also a catalyst for growth and maturity. As the novel ends, there is the suggestion that Rufus has added to his life a new dimension of self-awareness and perhaps even faith as a result of his father's death by automobile.

If the American dream is a dream of possession—of not merely owning things physically but of having mastery and control over them—then the peculiarly American nightmare is having possession without control. From the silent film comedies to *A Death In The Family*, the theme of the machine out of control has a long and ominous history in American life and literature. In the unsettling statistics of America's annual motor vehicle fatalities and in the works of writers like Fitzgerald, Faulkner, Hemingway, and Agee, the car has proved to be a problematical and less than compliant appendage to man. Whether the car is stymied by the natural elements (*The Reivers* and *A Farewell To Arms*), transformed into an instrument of death by careless drivers (*The Great Gatsby*), or a victim of its own mechanical aberrations, man's four-wheeled alter ego has proved to be a curse as well as a blessing. Yet for all the car's inconsistencies and unpredictability, the American has been reluctant to loosen his grip on the one possession above all others that holds him in thrall. Hence he goes on naming, humanizing, ritualizing, and deifying his car until it either "rides" him or goes out of control.

In our dreams of possession, then, as in those of youth, freedom, and success, the automobile has been a ubiquitous and important presence. For youth, cars open up the physical spaces beyond the neighborhood and metaphorical places beyond childish concerns and pastimes. In pursuing a dream of freedom, Americans look to the car as a practical means of finding the (impractical) liberation they seek. Freedom is the road beyond the last stop sign . . . and before the next one. To insure success, or to announce it, in a country where life is allegedly "a fluid, wide open race, winner take all," the car seems the ideal machine within which Americans can run—and win—that race in style. Finally, the American's dream of possession—of appropriating and mastering objects and making (or remaking) them in his own image—finds its most natural expression in the possession of a car.

When the automobile stops short, as indeed it must, of its inflated promise—when the neighborhood and the more mobile years beyond youth prove less satisfying than the ones left behind; when the road to freedom grows congested and blocked; when the price of success is dearer than its value; and when the possession either becomes possessor or races out of control—the automobile acts as a catalyst for the American nightmare.

Among our best writers and artists, the way out of the nightmare is not compromise or resignation, but escape into still another dream world. When real places become too treacherous to exist in, creative minds devise fictive spaces painstakingly stripped of terror and the machines that cause it. Ironically, however, once artists establish their mythical realms, they use them, as do Faulkner, Hawkes, Fitzgerald, Oldenburg, Agee, and others, to write, sculpt, or in some way express their feelings about the old dreams and nightmaeres they have left behind.

Whether a portion of America's automobile-linked dreams survives as an Edenic island (*Second Skin*), the impulse to keep running (*Rabbit, Run*), "a fresh, green breast of the new world" (*The Great Gatsby*), or a brilliant butterfly alighting on a coffin (*A Death In The Family*), a distinctive pattern emerges. In that pattern, the original American Dream is as dependent upon a car as the ensuing nightmare. The dream that survives the nightmare, however, is curiously bereft of any vehicles. Purged of its promise as well as its disappointment, the car no longer occupies center stage. Yet, like the ghost of an actress that earlier trod those same boards, the spectre of the car is never absent. In America, the automobile shapes—and haunts —the imagination.

NOTES

1. William Shakespeare, *King Lear*, II, iv.

2. Ralph Waldo Emerson, "Ode Inscribed to W. H. Channing," *Poems*, 1847.

3. Ernest Cassirer, *Language and Myth*, trans. Susanne K. Langer (New York: Harper & Bros., 1946; Dover Edition, 1953), p. 72.

4. Eric Partridge, *Slang Today and Yesterday*, 4th ed. (London: Routledge & Kegan Paul, Ltd., 1933), p. 315.

5. Hannah Campbell, *Why Did They Name It . . .* ? (New York: Fleet Publishing Corporation, Ace Books, 1964), p. 169. For a sentimental and amusing eulogy to the passing of the Model T, see Lee Strout White, "Farewell, My Lovely," *New Yorker*, May 16, 1936, pp. 20-22.

6. A graphic illustration of the strong link in men's minds between the horse and the car (early known as the "horseless carriage") can be seen in the work of the contemporary sculptor, Jason Seley. Using as his model the famous Donatello equestrian, which in its turn was modelled on the classical equestrian statue of Marcus Aurelius, Seley updates the concept of man on horseback by fashioning his schulpture, *Colleoni II* entirely out of automobile bumpers. See also recent advertisement for the Ford Mustang with an enlarged insert of the hood ornament, a wild mustang.

7. Fred Muir, *How To Keep Your VW Alive: A Manual of Step by Step Procedures For the Compleat Idiot* (Santa Fe, New Mexico: John Muir Publications, 1972).

8. Elaine May satirizes this kind of phenomenon in the brilliant opening sequence of her film, *A New Leaf*. A team of men in pristine white "doctors' coats" are debating a difficult diagnosis, while, in the background, a heart-monitoring machine registers an ominous graph. The hero, played by Walter Matthau, watches and waits nervously as the automotive mechanics conclude their diagnosis on his chronically ill Ferrari.

9. Kenneth Schneider, *Autokind Vs. Mankind*, pp. 20-23.

10. e. e. cummings, "XIX" in *Is 5, Complete Poems, 1913-1962* (New York: Harcourt Brace Jovanovich, Inc., 1972). The complete text is in the Appendix.

11. See Thorstein Veblen, *Theory of the Leisure Class: An Economic Study of Institutions* (New York: Vanguard Press, 1927), p. 28. Yet it is true that in a number of primitive African societies, ownership is a right reserved solely for women.

12.   William Faulkner, *Intruder In The Dust* (New York: Random House, 1948), p. 238.

13.   Thomas Pynchon, *V.* (Philadelphia: J. B. Lippincott Co., 1961; Bantam Books, 1964), pp. 18, 19.

14.   Ernst Cassirer, *Language and Myth*, p. 59.

15.   Andrew Greeley, "Myth, Symbols, and Rituals in the Modern World," *The Critic*, vol. 20, no. 3 (December 1961-January 1962); quoted in Mircea Eliade, *Myth and Reality*, trans. Willar R. Trask (New York: Harper & Row, 1963), p. 186. In KKTFSB, Tom Wolfe also makes a strong case for automobile worship, using a remarkably similar vocabulary.

16.   Harry Crews, *Car* (New York: William Morrow & Co., Inc., 1972), pp. 16, 18.

17.   Flannery O'Connor, *Wise Blood* (New York: Harcourt, Brace & World, 1952) in *3 by Flannery O'Connor* (New York: Signet Book, 1962), pp. 41, 43.

18.   See Preface to O'Connor, *Wise Blood*, p. 8.

19.   Flannery O'Connor, "The Life You Save May Be Your Own," in *A Good Man Is Hard To Find (New York: Harcourt, Brace, & World, 1955) in 3 by Flannery O'Connor*, p. 161.

20.   Norman Mailer, *Of A Fire On The Moon* (New York: Little, Brown & Co., 1969; Signet Edition, 1971), p. 403.

21.   Jean-Paul Sartre, *Being and Nothingness: An Essay On Phenomenological Ontology* (New York: Washington Square Press, 1966), p. 756.

22.   The burial of the Ford is reminiscent of the ancient pagan-/Christian burials afforded to royal persons and their possessions around the sixth and seventh centuries A.D. While the royal body usually was given Christian burial, vestiges of pagan tradition were enacted in the entombment of the possessions of the deceased in a symbolically adorned ship. (The ship, according to tradition, transported the belongings of the dead to the netherworld.) The most famous of these ship cenotaphs is the Sutton Hoo, unearthed on the English coast in 1939; see C. L. Wrenn, "Sutton Hoo and Beowulf," in *Anthology of Beowulf Criticism*, ed. Lewis E. Nicholson (Indiana: Univ. of Notre Dame Press, 1963), pp. 311-330.

23.   Hugh Kenner, "Art in a Closed Field," *Virginia Quarterly Review* (Autumn 1962), p. 599.

24.   Barbara Rose, *This Book About the Work of Claes Oldenburg Was Written By Barbara Rose For The Museum of Modern Art*

(Greenwich: New York Graphic Society, Ltd., 1970), p. 97. For pictures and detailed descriptions of *Autobodys*, see Michael Kirby, *Happenings* (New York: E. P. Dutton & Co., Inc., 1966), pp. 262-268.

25.   Rose, *This Book About the Work of Claes Oldenburg*, pp. 96, 99.

26.   Although his work differs from Oldenburg's, sculptor Ernest Trova is also preoccupied with the "subtle kinship" between technological objects and the human image. In his *Falling Man* series, Trova literally puts man on wheels (wheels at shoulders and ankles), suggesting that man and his car are one. Lawrence Alloway calls these figures "mechanomorphic" in *Trova: Selected Works, 1953-1966* (New York: Pace Gallery, 1966).

27.   Rose, *This Book About the Work of Claes Oldenburg*, p. 98.

28.   Ibid., p. 100

29.   Ibid., p. 96.

30.   Ibid. Similarly, in magical thinking, the person who possesses something of another man or god, be it knowledge of his name, his fingernail parings, or a representative image of him, is said to have "mastery over the being and will" of that figure. To hold sway or mastery may be interpreted as having the power to prevent that man or god from inflicting harm on the possessor.

31.   Schneider, *Autokind Vs. Mankind*, p. 37. Along the same lines, Charles "Engine" Wilson allegedly said, as late as the sixties, that what's good for General Motors is good for the rest of the country.

32.   Crews, *Car*, p. 53.

33.   James Agee, "Comedy's Greatest Era," James Agee Trust, 1949; reprinted in *Film: An Anthology*, ed. Daniel Talbot (New York: Simon & Schuster, Inc., 1959), p. 148.

34.   Ibid., pp. 149-150.

35.   James Agee, *A Death in the Family* (New York: Grosset and Dunlap, Inc., 1967; Bantam Books, 1969). In his March 2, 1948 and May 11, 1955 letters to his friend and former teacher, Father Flye, Agee makes reference to his work in progress on what ultimately became *A Death In The Family;* see *Letters of James Agee to Father Flye* (New York: George Braziller, Inc., 1962; Bantam, 1963), pp. 156, 210.

36.   William Frohock says of *A Death In The Family* that its "selecting, narrating vision moves through scene after scene, like the lens of a camera directed by someone who knows what the directors of old silent films had to know if they were to survive: how to narrate

visually" (*The Novel of Violence In America* [Dallas: Southern
Methodist University Press, 1950, 1957], p. 229).

37.   Although the essay was not a part of the manuscript which
Agee left, a note preceding the text reads, "the editors would certainly
have urged him to include it in the final draft."

Appendix A

GOIN' DOWN THE ROAD

by *Woody Guthrie*

Well I'm goin' down this old dusty road, road, road
Yes I'm goin' down this old dusty road
Yes I'm goin' down this old dusty road, road, road
And I ain't gonna be treated this way!

I'm goin' where them dust storms never blow
I'm goin' where them dust storms never blow
I'm goin' where them dust storms never blow, blow, blow
'Cause I ain't gonna be treated this a way!

My children need three square meals a day, day, day
Yes my children need three square meals a day
Oh my children need three square meals a day, day, day
And I ain't gonna be treated this a way!

They say I'm a dustbowl refugee, refugee,
Yes they say I'm a dustbowl refugee
Oh they say I'm a dustbowl refugee, refugee
But I ain't gonna be treated this a way!

Takes a ten dollar shoe to fit my feet, feet, feet,
Takes a ten dollar shoe to fit my feet
I said a ten dollar shoe fits my feet, feet, feet,
But I ain't gonna be treated this a way!

Your two dollar shoe hurts my feet, feet, feet,
Your two dollar shoe hurts my feet
Yes your two dollar shoe hurts my feet, feet, feet
But I ain't gonna be treated this a way!

Yes I'm goin' where them grapes and peaches grow, grow, grow
I'm goin' where them grapes an' peaches grow
Oh I'm goin' where them grapes and peaches grow, grow, grow
'Cause I ain't gonna be treated this a way!

I'm gonna change this damned old world around, round, round
I'm gonna change this damned old world around,
Yes I'm gonna change this damned old world around, round, round
'Cause I ain't gonna be treated this a way!

"Going Down the Road
(I Ain't Going To Be Treated This Way)"
Words and Music by Woody Guthrie and Lee Hays
TRO - © Copyright 1960 and 1963 HOLLIS MUSIC, INC.,
New York, N.Y. Used by permission.

Appendix B

"XIX"

by e. e. cummings

she being Brand

-new;and you
know consequently a
little stiff i was
careful of her and(having

thoroughly oiled the universal
joint tested my gas felt of
her radiator made sure her springs were O.

K.)i went right to it flooded-the-carburetor cranked her

up.slipped the
clutch and then somehow got into reverse she
kicked what
the hell)next
minute i was back in neutral tried and

again slo-wly;bare,ly nudg.   ing(my

lev-er Right-
oh and her gears being in
A 1 shape passed

from low through
second-in-to-high like
greasedlightning)just as we turned the corner of Divinity

avenue i touched the accelerator and give

her the juice,good

          (it
was the first ride and believe i we was
happy to see how nice she acted right up to
the last minute coming back down by the Public
Gardens i slammed on
the

internalexpanding
&
externalcontracting
brakes Bothatonce and

brought allofher tremB

-ling
to a:dead.

stand-
; Still)

Selected Bibliography

Adams, Henry. *The Education of Henry Adams*. Boston, Mass.: Houghton Mifflin Co., 1918; Sentry Edition, 1961.

Agee, James. *A Death In The Family*. New York: Grosset & Dunlap, Inc., 1967; Bantam Books, 1969.

Anderson, Rudolph E. *The Story Of The American Automobile: Highlights and Sidelights*. Washington, D.C.: Public Affairs Press, 1950.

Appleton, Victor Jr. *Tom Swift And His Electric Runabout or The Speediest Car On The Road*. New York: Grosset & Dunlap, 1910.

Bellamy, Edward. *Looking Backward: 2000-1887*. 1888; reprint ed., New York: Signet Classic, 1960.

Boorstin, Daniel J. *The Image: A Guide to Pseudo-Events in America*. New York: Harper & Row, 1961.

Campbell, Hannah. *Why Did They Name It . . . ?* New York: Ace Books, 1964.

Cassirer, Ernst. *Language And Myth*. Translated by Susanne K. Langer. New York: Harper & Bros., 1946; Dover Edition, 1953.

Crews, Harry. *Car*. New York: William Morrow & Co., Inc., 1972.

Crowther, George. *Sanitized For Your Protection*. London: Secher & Warburg, 1966.

Cook, Bruce. *The Beat Generation*. New York: Charles Scribner's Sons, 1971.

Cruz, Victor Hernandez. *Snaps*. New York: Random House; Vintage Books, 1969.

cummings, e. e. *Complete Poems 1913-1962*. New York: Harcourt Brace Jovanovich, Inc., 1972.

Dos Passos, John. *The Big Money: Third In The Trilogy U.S.A.*, 1933. Boston: Houghton Mifflin Co, 1946; Signet Classics, 1969.

Farber, Stephen. *"Graffiti* Ranks With *Bonnie and Clyde." The New York Times*, 5 August 1973.

Faulkner, William. *The Town.* New York: Curtis Publishing Co., 1957; Vintage Books, 1957.

    The Reivers: A Reminiscence. New York: Random House, 1962; Vintage Books, 1962.

Felson, Henry Gregor. *Hot Rod.* 20th ed. New York: E. P. Dutton & Co., Inc., 1950.

Fiedler, Leslie. *Love And Death In The American Novel.* New York: Dell Publishing Co., Inc., 1960, 1967.

Fitzgerald, F. Scott. *The Great Gatsby.* New York: Charles Scribner's Sons, 1925; reprint ed., 1953.

Hassan, Ihab. *Radical Innocence: Studies In The Contemporary American Novel.* New Jersey: Princeton Univ. Press, 1961.

Hawkes, John. *Second Skin.* New York: New Directions, 1963, 1964.

Holmes, John Clellon. *Nothing More To Declare.* New York: E. P. Dutton & Co., Inc., 1967.

Kennedy, X. J. "An Appreciative Essay." In *Hardening Rock.* Edited by Bruce L. Chipman. Boston: Little, Brown & Co., 1972.

Kerouac, Jack. *On The Road.* New York: The Viking Press, Inc., 1957; Signet, 1960.

Kirby, Michael. *Happenings.* New York: E. P. Dutton & Co., Inc., 1966.

Knebel, Fletcher. *Dark Horse.* New York: Doubleday & Co., Inc., 1972.

Kouwenhoven, John. *Made in America: The Arts In Modern Civilization.* Newton Centre, Mass.: Charles T. Branford Co., 1948.

Lynn, Kenneth. *The Dream Of Success: A Study Of The Modern American Imagination.* Boston: Little, Brown & Co., 1955.

Mc Murtry, Larry, *The Last Picture Show.* New York: Dell Publishing Co., Inc., 1966.

Mailer, Norman. *Of A Fire On The Moon.* New York: Little, Brown & Co., 1969; Signet Edition, 1971.

Marx, Leo. *The Machine In The Garden: Technology And The Pastoral Ideal.* London: Oxford Univ. Press, 1964.

Mumford, Lewis. *The Highway And The City.* New York: Harcourt, Brace & World, Inc., 1963.

Nabokov, Vladimir. *Lolita.* Olympia Press, 1955; Berkley Medallion Books, 1966.

O'Connor, Flannery. "The Life You Save May Be Your Own." In *3 By Flannery O'Connor*. New York: Signet Books, 1962.

————. *Wise Blood,* In *3 By Flannery O'Connor*. New York: Signet Books, 1962.

Olson, Charles, *Call Me Ishmael.* San Francisco: City Lights, 1947.

Pynchon, Thomas. *V.* Philadelphia: J. B. Lippincott Co., 1961; Bantam Books, 1964.

Reed, J. D. *Expressways.* New York: Simon & Schuster, 1969.

Rose, Barbara. *This Book About The Work Of Claes Oldenburg Was Written By Barbara Rose For The Museum Of Modern Art.* Greenwich, Conn.: New York Graphic Society, Ltd., 1970.

Rosenbaum, Jean. *Is Your Volkswagen A Sex Symbol?* New York: Hawthorn Books, Inc., 1972; Bantam Books, 1973.

Sartre, Jean Paul. *Being And Nothingness: An Essay On Phenomenological Ontology.* Translated by Hazel E. Barnes. New York: Simon & Schuster, Inc., Washington Square Press, 1966.

Schneider, Kenneth R. *Autokind Vs. Mankind.* New York: W. W. Norton & Co., Inc., 1971.

Selby, Hubert Jr. *Last Exit To Brooklyn.* New York: Grove Press, Inc., 1957.

Simpson, Louis. *At The End Of The Open Road.* Middleton, Conn.: Wesleyan Univ. Press, 1960.

Steinbeck, John. *The Grapes of Wrath.* New York: The Viking Press, Inc., 1939; Bantam Books, 1970.

————. *Travels With Charley: In Search Of America.* New York: The Viking Press, Inc., 1962; Bantam Books, 1962.

Tanner, Tony. *City Of Words: American Fiction 1950-1970.* New York: Harper & Row, 1971.

Tractenberg, Alan. *Brooklyn Bridge: Fact And Symbol.* New York: Oxford Univ. Press, 1965.

Updike, John. *Rabbit Redux.* New York: Alfred A. Knopf, Inc., 1971; Fawcett Crest, 1972.

————. *Rabbit, Run.* New York; Alfred A. Knopf, Inc., 1960; Fawcett Crest, 1974.

Weesner, Theodore, *The Car Thief.* New York: Random House, Inc., 1967, 1972.

White, Lee Strout. "Farewell, My Lovely." *New Yorker*, 16 May 1936, pp. 20-22.

Williams, Mason. "Autobiography." *Flavors.* New York: Doubleday & Co., Inc., 1964.

Wolfe, Tom. "The Kandy*Kolored Tangerine*Flake Streamline Baby." *The Kandy*Kolored Tangerine*Flake Streamline Baby.* New York: Farrar, Straus & Giroux, 1965; Pocket Books, 1966.

Zukofsky, Louis. *Ferdinand.* London: Jonathan Cape, Ltd., 1968.

Index